Sujal

Thanks for
being on the
"Blue"
work!

good

Steve Howell
May 2, 2011

AHEAD *of the* CURVE

A Guide to Applied Strategic Thinking

Steven J. Stowell, Ph.D.
Stephanie S. Mead

CMOE Press
Salt Lake City, UT

CMOE, Inc.
9146 South 700 East
Sandy, UT 84070

ISBN # 0-9724627-3-2

First Edition
Fifth Printing, August 2010

Editing: Helen Hodgson, Martha Rice, Deb Hedgepeth, Cherissa Newton, and Debbie Stowell
Cover Design: Cohezion
Graphic Design: Design Type Service

This book and other CMOE publications are available by ordering direct from the publisher.

CMOE Press
(801) 569-3444
www.cmoe.com

ACKNOWLEDGMENTS

This book certainly wouldn't have been possible without the dedication and support of our invaluable contributors, to whom we wish to dedicate this book:

- Our incredibly talented design team—Martha Rice, Deb Hedgepeth, and Cherissa Newton—who all played central roles in sharpening the manuscripts and making the book a reality. We thank them for their encouragement and hard work.

- The exceptional CMOE team, who are true ambassadors of our ideas and are always willing to experiment with us.

- Our clients, who inspire us and provide creative input as we apply and refine these ideas.

- The participants in our workshops, from whom we have had the good fortune of being able to learn.

- Helen Hodgson, our diligent editor. We appreciate her talents and input.

- Our extraordinary families who were so patient with us when our minds were working overtime on these skills and concepts. They give us the strength to do what we do.

CONTENTS

PREFACE

You may find this book a little different from most books on strategy. Nearly all the information we have found on strategy centers on corporate or national strategy. This book focuses entirely on you, the individual, as well as your immediate team.

You see, most organizations have made great strides in empowering employees. They have encouraged people to take initiative, to make a difference, to be more entrepreneurial, and to get closer to the customer. There is no doubt that more decision making and responsibility have been pushed deeper within organizations, so that everyone is expected to be a manager. However, with all of these improvements, organizations have done little to sharpen people's skills to think and act like leaders, strategically within their own realm of responsibility. Strategic leaders lay the groundwork for tomorrow's opportunities. This is why we believe that practical and personal strategic thinking skills need to be developed. This book is dedicated to helping people not only learn how to think strategically, but also how to become a strategic force in their own work, career, team, or life – how to truly ignite change for the better.

> "In order to make a fire burn, you fan live coals. In order to keep your organization fired up, it's imperative that you find and motivate the leaders or potential leaders in your organization regardless of how far down the line they might be."
>
> *Dexter Yager*

 A truly strategic person is someone with the courage and foresight to solve tomorrow's problems today. He or she can anticipate and exploit tomorrow's opportunities now. Let's face it: tomorrow's solutions won't be discovered with today's short term tactical thinking. We believe people can and should live more strategically. Thus, our book will explore how to think, plan, and act more strategically at the individual level and on the front lines of work.

Some people in senior positions may say, "We don't want strategic thinkers in our organization. We need 'doers.' Strategy formulation is something we do in the ivory tower." We don't think that these executives need to worry; creating an army of good strategic thinkers won't make organizations weaker. On the contrary, an organization full of people who think ahead of the curve will be stronger because it will head off problems before they surface and maximize future productivity. We believe everyone needs to think about how they can adapt to a changing environment to add greater value. This transition will occur through bottom-up strategy. Rest assured, good strategic thinkers won't turn the workforce into reckless rebels. In fact, strategic thinking at the working level requires a link to organization strategy (if one is in place) in order to work at its best.

> "Individual commitment to a group effort – that is what makes a team work, a company work, a society work, a civilization work."
>
> Vincent Thomas "Vince" Lombardi, NFL Football Coach

In the chapters ahead we will carefully but simply explain each strategic thinking skill or element. We will share practical examples and illustrate how each of the strategic thinking competencies works. We will also provide specific suggestions and activities for developing your own personal strategic thinking skills. Like any good tool, each skill or step in the process has specific uses and the potential for misuse. To avoid misuse, you will be given cautions to keep in mind as you explore these skills.

What follows are some suggestions for making the reading of this book more beneficial for you. Treat this material as food for thought, and keep a pen handy so you can highlight key tips and make notes in the space available. As you think about these skills, consider how you can best apply them to yourself, your current work, and your organization or team. If you find yourself struggling with some of the concepts or having difficulties applying the skills, give us a phone call and we would be happy to discuss, clarify, or further explain anything in the book. Remember, you are your own best expert about your work and your future, so don't hesitate to adapt, ad-lib, or adjust the material to fit your reality and your environment. One of the keys to mapping out your future is to discover ideas, principles, and skills that apply to your situation. If you discover that the whole process is too much to apply at once, pick and choose parts that work for you now and gradually add more as you go.

The power of applied strategic thinking is finding the best way to incorporate these tools into your unique environment. Have fun as you contemplate your personal future and as you begin to chart your destiny and journey into the future.

> "If you don't have a plan (goals) for what you want, then you will probably find yourself buying into someone else's plan and later find out that wasn't the direction you wanted to go. You've got to be the architect of your life."
>
> *Jim Rohn*
> *Philosopher*

CHAPTER ONE

Introduction to
Applied Strategic Thinking

1

Introduction to Applied Strategic Thinking

W
e have always had an interest in historical events, military campaigns, politics, and global business strategy. Many valuable lessons can be learned from political forces and from the rise and fall of corporations and nations. Yet as interesting as these topics are, they still leave us and many other individuals a little empty when it comes to answering questions like: What does it mean for me and the way I manage my career, my team, and my life? Why do some individuals advance in their careers and others fall back? What causes great leaders to emerge from the technical world successfully while others languish?

When it comes to the grand corporate stage, practical and applied thinking seems to be missing from the formula. People on the front lines and in the trenches should be equally smart and strategically intuitive within their own sphere of responsibilities. Looking at history, we find that the decisions and actions of unknown, everyday, front-line leaders made a decisive difference. These people tipped the scales, creating the turning point in great battles, great innovations, or in the political careers of famous leaders.

Clearly, it is entertaining and informative to read about what CEOs at Samsung, GE, Sony, Chrysler, or Southwest Airlines are

> "Strategy without tactics is the slowest route to victory. Tactics without strategy is the noise before defeat."
>
> *Sun Tzu*
> *c. 490 BC*
> *Chinese Military*
> *Strategist*

doing to be more competitive and strategic. However, though most of us will probably not become captains of mega corporations, leaders, and individual contributors, we could be better at our craft by applying a bit of strategic thinking to our environments. While we won't individually compete head-to-head like the in-dustrial giants do, we do compete against unseen  and formidable adversaries like complacency, obsolescence, me-diocrity, reactivity, inefficiency, waste, and rigidity. Every day we go into battle, struggle to out-maneuver and stay ahead of changes, figure out how to bring more value to our function, and win over these hidden foes. Our strategic victories won't make newspaper headlines, for sure, but the personal stakes are just as important. We must prevail, or we put personal success and security at risk. To survive, each of us needs to be as tenacious and entrepreneur-ial about our own situation as Jack Welch was about his success with GE. We are not suggesting that a person become more ma-nipulative, deceptive, or strictly self-interested. On the contrary, we are talking about maximizing and optimizing your personal contribution to the common good of your organization or busi-ness unit. Well-thought-out, personal applied strategy is the best way for you to become a better team player and better performer. Improving your team position makes the entire organization more competitive. We strongly believe people in any part of the organi-zation hierarchy can and should work at getting better by com-peting and achieving their own strategic goals and not by beating up on others or behaving in an insidious, competitive fashion with colleagues and cohorts.

Certainly lessons can be gleaned from the corporate planning titans of the world, les-sons that can give us some insights into achieving more, doing more, contributing more, and being more. But what we are talk-ing about isn't the planning per se, although

"Our focus is how to think more broadly and long term."

planning is part of it. Our focus is how to think more broadly and long term. It is about clarifying what you want, what you will produce in the future, what motivates you, who you serve in the future, and how to be more innovative. So, if you  want to gain advantage in a way that will help your team or organization conquer future challenges, this book can help.

We live and operate in a fast-paced, turbulent environment with many uncertainties, hazards, and opportunities. With a little discipline and thought, we have the ability to gain, expand, and exercise greater influence over our work and life. We also have the capacity to understand, control, and predict our environment better. We can be a more potent force if we will but follow a few simple guidelines that will lead to creative solutions to our strategic problems and enable us to achieve our objectives while conserving our resources. After all, isn't thinking strategically a key component in living well and optimizing performance at a personal and team level? Simply put, everyone must be more entrepreneurial and competitive as we move into the future. We must be willing to improve on the status quo, tackle the forces that work against our future success, and better harness the positive forces and levers that are on our side.

> "Victorious warriors win first and then go to war, while defeated warriors go to war first and then seek to win."
>
> Sun Tzu
> "Strategic Assessments
> Art of War"

The meaning of all of this hit home one day when a CEO of a large global corporation shared with one of our classes what he believed was the key to the organization's future. He said, "Everyone in the organization has to be a contributor (not just a performer). This means you have to be better at what you do than the person doing your same work in competitor organizations." If we are to outperform our competitors, if we are to stay ahead of obsolescence, if we want to be effective in our work tomorrow, we have to adopt a more strategic perspective today. We have to be more innovative, to anticipate, recognize, and leverage change and opportunities so that they produce benefits in our individual work over the long haul.

"Everyone in the organization has to be a contributor (not just a performer). This means you have to be better at what you do than the person doing your same work in competitor organizations."

The organization's success is dependent on each individual's ability to contribute to the whole and become more valuable to the organization and society. Clearly, organizations want people who can **act**: routinely execute activities and tasks efficiently; but, organizations will also need people who can **think**: look ahead, anticipate change, invent new solutions, outmaneuver disasters before they arrive, avert a crisis, or find ways to streamline work methods. They are looking for everyone to invest in their work. In fact, we like to refer to it as "every employee an entrepreneur" in his or her own function or field of operation.

So when we talk about applied strategic thinking, our focus is the grass roots. We are not talking about simply **involving** individual members in the formulation of broad organizational strategies. Rather, we are talking about real strategy for the manager or team itself, about turning everyone into an individual strategist. While individual contributors, team members, and leaders should be involved in and consulted on grand corporate strategy, this book is designed to help individuals discover greater success for themselves and their teams in harmony with the organization and with other teams. We believe that organizations today are too complex and too large to survive on "top-down" strategy alone. They need bottom-up strategy to blend and synchronize with strategy that cascades down from the top.

Let us be extremely clear in saying; we are not suggesting that everyone take off in his or her own direction—hardly! What we are talking about is individuals seeing the organization and their internal customers clearly and becoming totally aligned with and supportive of the organization's strategy and mission.

Applied strategic thinking is all about helping individual contributors and managers "put the fire hose down" and step back from the daily activity, discover what strategy means to them personally, and ask some basic questions:

- Why am I doing these activities?
- Who am I serving?
- Do I know what my internal customers, partners, or key stakeholders will want from me in the future?
- What is my informal agreement and understanding "contract" with my team?
- How well am I delivering results and outputs?
- How can I add more distinctive value to the organization?
- How is my environment changing, and what does that change mean to me?
- How will my role change in the future?
- How can I better prepare myself for the future so that I do not become obsolete and irrelevant?
- How can I better read (interpret) the environment and make a reasonable forecast about what lies ahead?
- What can I do now that is different and yet will produce a payoff in the future?
- What will be the truly important value-added projects and tasks?

By and large these questions represent an important and different thought process than most people are familiar with. Applied strategic thinking is simply a guide to help you "jump start" your strategic thought process; about how you can add value to your organization in the long term. It is a road map to stimulate your thinking and help guide you through your individual strategy formulation process quickly and easily.

So if you are looking for skills, advice, and insights gleaned from the latest and greatest airline company, technology company, or successful government program, this book won't do it for you. But if you want to help yourself or teach others how to develop strategic thinking and become more successful in the journey of life, you have definitely come to the right place. It is never too late to begin acting strategically.

> "The will to win is important, but the will to prepare is vital."
>
> *Joe Paterno*
> *American College Football Coach*

CHAPTER TWO

Strategic Landscape

2

Strategic Landscape

The word "strategy" is used loosely by many people and in the writings of various authors. It means different things to different people. Sometimes strategy is defined as a plan and sometimes as a future goal.

For us, being strategic means being an active force in creating and shaping your future. According to this definition, strategy is very personal. It boils down to seeing the future and creating choices for yourself. When you don't have choices, you are locked into responding with robot-like tactical action. Being strategic means having the desire and capability to help create the future of your choosing and not limiting yourself to forces and dynamics that act upon you.

> "The people who get on in this world are the people who get up and look for circumstances they want, and, if they can't find them, make them."
>
> *George Bernard Shaw, "Mrs. Warren's Profession," Act II (1893)*

To help you understand what we mean, think of yourself in entrepreneurial terms, as if you were a large corporation. To be successful, organizations have to be in the business of solving customer problems and providing valued solutions. Long-term survival depends on having the right business model, being agile and adaptable, utilizing smart marketing, and becoming a partner with the consumer. It is all about creating value now and in the future. Applied strategic thinking focuses this same skill and spirit on a personal level, regardless of your job, position, or rank in an organization. Smart individuals discover their personal business model and adjust it to meet changes in the environment.

The whole point is that you can be more effective if you look to the future and think about where you are headed and what you want to accomplish. You have a strategic landscape where you can map out and visualize your world from a strategic perspective, as depicted in the following graph:

> "Drive thy business, let it not drive thee."
> *Benjamin Franklin*
> *American Writer and*
> *Statesman*

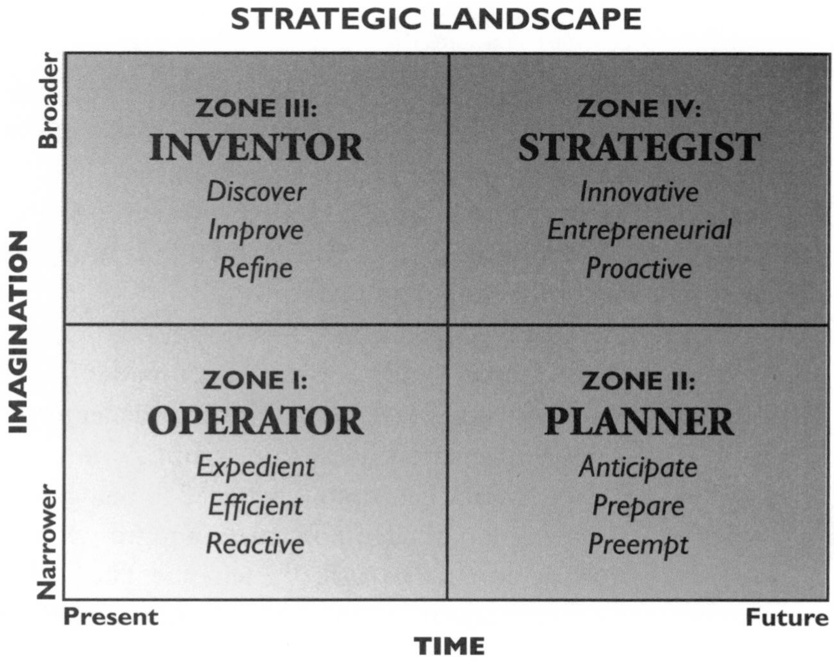

STRATEGIC LANDSCAPE

ZONE III:	**ZONE IV:**
INVENTOR	**STRATEGIST**
Discover	*Innovative*
Improve	*Entrepreneurial*
Refine	*Proactive*
ZONE I:	**ZONE II:**
OPERATOR	**PLANNER**
Expedient	*Anticipate*
Efficient	*Prepare*
Reactive	*Preempt*

Vertical axis (IMAGINATION): Broader (top) / Narrower (bottom)

Horizontal axis (TIME): Present (left) / Future (right)

The horizontal axis on the chart represents the time dimension of strategy, ranging from the present to the future. We have found that when most people think about strategy, they are thinking about this axis, planning for and anticipating the future. But the other element of the strategic landscape is the level of imagination represented on the vertical axis with a range from narrow to broad.

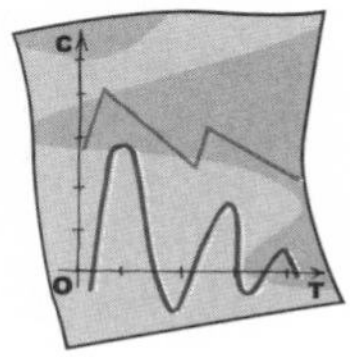

Zone I: OPERATOR

Most of us try to be excellent at performing our present, primary function and don't get a lot of time for strategic thought. Some people feel like operational robots in their jobs: stiff, mechanical, and not very imaginative. It is like having an 800 pound gorilla on your back. If you find yourself in this situation, you are probably caught in Zone I, OPERATOR. Like most people, you have probably figured out how to efficiently execute the immediate tasks you are faced with. In fact, you may believe that fulfilling these functions is really all you have the time, resources, and energy to do.

Too often we get caught up in this zone and can't escape its magnetic pull; to get outside the "present" moment. We refer to the daunting task of reining in operational pressures as "taming the beast." The beast or 800 pound gorilla represents the regular tasks, urgencies, and responsibilities that easily fill up your time and keep you from becoming more strategic.

To truly be strategic you need to move beyond the narrow focus of the "working harder syndrome" into the broader future. Find the time to move outside this box and think in broader terms.

 Even momentarily escaping from Zone I isn't an easy task because we get used to being busy, having too much on our plate, and functioning on an adrenaline rush. Einstein said it best when he stated that the definition of insanity is doing the same thing over and over again and expecting a different result in the future. Because caging the gorilla can be challenging to do, we have dedicated an entire chapter to specific skills needed to propel you away from the operational magnet and into a "strategic zone."

Zone II: PLANNER

The next level of the landscape is Zone II: PLANNER. This is where you start to act strategically because you are looking forward and anticipating the future. However, the scope may be too

narrow to maximize your full strategic potential. This doesn't mean you won't find strategic benefit being a planner; it is certainly a good place to start. At this level of the strategic landscape, you are looking further ahead in the context of your current routine. In this zone you are moving outside your box in terms of the future but without the benefit of a little innovation.

In Zone II you will indeed find opportunities to be what we call "pre-active," but not truly "pro-active." In this part of the strategic landscape, you might be asking yourself questions like "What kind of staffing needs will I have if my work load continues to increase in my current department?" "Where do I want my current team to be in the next few

> What's the use of running if you are not on the right road?
>
> *German Proverb*

months?" or "When can I introduce my existing services to other divisions?" A very simple example might be the life of a key piece of equipment. Experience tells you that it is bound to die in a few months, so you think about a replacement piece of equipment now. Here, in Zone II, you are on a strategic path because you are thinking ahead from a "time" perspective.

Now you need to orient your mind to think about the future and how your ideas, decision, and actions today will impact it. Zone II: PLANNER is something a few people already are, but most find it uncomfortable and ambiguous to look into the future, even though they can probably predict future eventualities better than anyone else. They find comfort in just worrying about the here and now. Providing simple or quiet leadership and staying ahead of the game means diligently and consistently scanning the environment and surveying your own responsibilities, tasks, projects, and assignments, as well as being ready to turn change in the environment into an advantage. The first step is to follow a process, invest some

> "No great thing is created suddenly, any more than a bunch of grapes or a fig. If you tell me that you desire a fig, I answer that there must be time. Let it first blossom, then bear fruit, then ripen."
>
> *Epictetus*
> *Roman Philosopher*

time to free the mind to be a planner, and anticipate things that will provide the opening for strategic thought to blossom.

Zone III: INVENTOR

Zone III of the landscape is called IN-VENTOR. It is when strategic thinking is taken in a different direction because you are thinking creatively about the future, being innovative, and making value-added improvements that will help you be more effective. In this zone, you are doing things differently and better. Inventing innovative services or ways to work does not require large-scale flashes of genius. It is simply a way of searching and asking a few provocative questions such as "Where do I want to go with this project?", "How can I deliver a better solution to my internal and external customers?" or "Who will be my customer in the future?"

The answer to these questions may come quickly or in increments. Little innovative ideas build on each other until the pieces fit together to produce a comprehensive strategic picture. Some people take these steps deliberately and systematically, and some people function informally, by osmosis, new ideas and imagination flowing freely. Unfortunately, others don't have a clue; they either fall asleep at the wheel or prefer to stay in the reactive-defensive mode, which is basically being in Zone I.

> "Imagination is more important than knowledge."
>
> *Albert Einstein*
> *Theoretical Physicist*

One of the most serious impediments to working more creatively and strategically is believing the myth that people are born with a gift for innovation. This belief may be due in part to the perception that innovation requires blockbuster ideas and new gadgets or

gigantic inventions that change the course of history. Actually, strategic innovation is much simpler, easily within the grasp of anyone who has a desire to learn. Certainly, a climate for innovation within an organization is a big factor. It is helpful when the system in which you work reinforces being an inventor at the individual level. Regardless, you may at times feel vulnerable and exposed, while we believe that the critical factor at the personal and practical level is your willingness to work out the issues that may be blocking or limiting innovative thinking. As we touched on earlier, every organization needs as many people as possible to both think in strategically innovative terms and execute operationally. You must recognize and exploit opportunities within your sphere of influence to bring new innovations to the table.

> "You must recognize and exploit opportunities within your sphere of influence to bring new innovations to the table."

In a complex world, there is no way that a few leaders or a few smart people can do all the strategic inventing an organization needs. Innovations and long-term improvements have to come from a myriad of individuals. As these ideas begin to flow and mature, people can redeploy their resources, energy, efforts, and skills to take full advantage of innovative opportunities. The result is enhanced productivity, which enables the organization and its people to compete and prosper.

Zone IV: STRATEGIST

We call the final zone STRATEGIST, because this is the land of strategic opportunity. It is truly a blend of thinking both broad and long term. Here you will find the most valuable strategic breakthroughs, the ones that will lead to your long-term success. Zone IV is where you act as a strategist by thinking about the future in entrepreneurial ways. Here strategic thinking efforts are applied to things that are sustainable, distinctive, and extremely value added.

> "Good strategic thinkers in Zone IV have an uncanny ability to anticipate, recognize, and convert changes into opportunities."

Simply put, it is the way you creatively solve tomorrow's problems today and shape the future the way you want.

Good strategists in Zone IV have an uncanny ability to anticipate, recognize, and convert changes into opportunities. They understand that long-term change is the fuel for progress on their strategic journey. Success in a strategic sense is the ability to capitalize on and exploit change, to turn change to your advantage. This means being able to perpetuate yourself (or your team) and discover special ways of contributing. To enhance your unique contributions to the organization, you must be on the cutting edge of new ideas and innovations that allow you to deliver distinctive results in better ways and with greater efficiency in the future, not just the present.

In fact, strategy is all about improving your position to make a difference in the organization. If you don't make a difference or add value, or if you allow yourself to become irrelevant to the organization's fundamental mission, you will likely fail in the long run. The way to avoid failure or elimination from the game is to continually reinvent who you are, what you do, how you do it, and for whom you do it. Change provides the catalyst for this reinvention to occur and enables you to play a more significant role in the organization. You need the ability to manage, spark, work with, and harness change because it can be the greatest ally on a strategic journey.

When we refer to applied strategy, we are not saying that it has to be a grand, system-wide, revolutionary strategic change. Rather, breakthroughs can be subtle and quiet, without a lot of fanfare, hoop-la, or hype. In fact, being a strategist in Zone IV of the landscape is taking advantage of change that could be very personal, private, and internal. Examples include electing to alter

your perspective or attitude about customers, deciding to learn a new skill or technique, or noticing that a new member of the team has some special talents and capabilities worth learning. These are all small but strategic moves that will improve your position or avoid obsolescence. As you can imagine, the ability to see change developing gives strategists a distinctive edge because they can uncover new ideas, prove their value, and repeatedly move ahead of the curve.

Strategists know that the marketplace for their services and skills is always changing. Internal and external customers' needs and preferences change, the business plans of your manager or business unit are routinely updated, technology is always advancing, and suppliers and co-workers come and go. When change occurs, you have two choices. You can dismiss it and say, "Oh well, isn't that interesting. Things are always changing around here, and it doesn't seem like the right hand knows what the left hand is doing." Or you can be a strategist and say, "You know, I think I can see some things I can learn from our new manager," or "I need to consider if this new supplier will deliver as fast as our old  one did. Maybe I will do some checking into this," or "I wonder how we can take advantage of the new healthcare policy that was just announced." The choice is clear. You can be strategic and proactive about change, learning to adapt or create new solutions; or you can let the change "swamp your boat" and pull you under, screaming and yelling, and playing the role of a "victim."

THE FEAR OF STRATEGIC CHANGE

It is unfortunate, but too many people fear change. They fear the unknown and will go to great lengths mentally to avoid or deny it. Certainly some "harsh realities" are usually associated with change, which makes it natural to perceive an unknown as a threat to the security and balance that you have worked to achieve in Zone I. If you know how to manage change, it can produce winners; if you don't, change produces losers.

Reactive, short-term, purely operational executors, who live in Zone I, stand to lose a lot. Their only choice is to hunker down and hope the change blows over quickly with minimal damage. Sometimes tactical thinkers get caught in what is described as the "approach-avoidance" no-man's land. That is, they want to change at one moment and then, at the next moment, they seem to back off and retreat to familiar patterns of action. It is an exhausting back-and-forth phenomenon of "charge ahead" followed by a fall back and retreat stance. This pattern is fueled by irrational and often inaccurate assessments and predictions of the real risks, changing vs. standing still and doing nothing. Ultimately, their internal self-talk convinces them that they are better off and safer staying put a little longer in the security of Zone I. In short, they actually talk themselves out of exploiting an opportunity for a whole host of what we perceive as legitimate reasons: i.e., the timing isn't just right, the opportunity needs to be studied more, the budget is short, etc. The result is an endless cycle of rationalization and excuses. You name it, they can come up with every reason under the sun to stall and resist change.

> "You can't have a better tomorrow if you are thinking about yesterday all the time."
>
> *Charles F. Kettering*
> *American Electrical*
> *Engineer and*
> *Inventor*

Resistance to change is often so subtle and insidious that you don't even realize when you are caught in its grip. You convince yourself that resistance is totally logical and that valid reasons exist for <u>not</u> getting cracking and jumping through the window of opportunity and moving into the land of opportunity. Most of us are born with a healthy "change immune system," and because change often involves initial pain, our natural defenses kick in to

protect us and our sense of security. No opportunity comes along without some risks, and change never serves up a perfect fit with the current world (Zone I). You must make adjustments in your life. In effect, you have to cut, saw, and chisel to make the window of opportunity fit. In this process, you will encounter some bumps and bruises. It isn't easy. So what is the alternative? Remaining static while competitors or substitutes take easy shots at you doesn't make sense. If you remain static, you risk obsolescence. People who are consistently successful know how to adapt and have developed the discipline to cope. It is something we can all learn to do a little better if we choose.

You simply need to monitor and track the changes that occur in (1) your relationships with your colleagues and partners; (2) your work practices and processes; (3) your resources, tools, and technology; (4) your services; (5) your customers' situations; and (6) your bottom line performance (results). These 6 areas provide a valuable springboard for long-term success. Too many people hear the knock of opportunity (change) but fail to open the door and do something about it. They would rather shut themselves in and try to play it safe. Yet we know this is a slow, sure road to extinction. No one can prosper by isolating or insulating himself or herself from change.

If you recognize that change is coming, see needs emerge, and gradually redirect your efforts and resources, you can achieve an advantage, differentiating and transforming yourself from the  masses of people who wait around to be told what to do. You can learn to recognize every need and redeploy your efforts and resources. Who really wants to be behind in the game? Why not be entrepreneurial and proactive? At least you can be aware of what is happening, even if you don't have the power or formal approval to act as much as you would like. Awareness and information put you in a position to assume informal strategic leadership. It may take a

while before others are ready to act and convert change into opportunities, but they will come to value your leadership and insights.

Sometimes you may find that you are off track with your
estimates, but remember you also have to take some educated risks.

Machiavelli captured it well when he said:

It must be remembered that there is nothing more difficult to plan, more
doubtful of success, nor more dangerous to manage than the creation of
a new system.

And let it be noted that there is no more delicate matter to take in hand,
nor more dangerous to conduct, nor more doubtful in its success, than
to set up as a leader in the introduction of changes.

For he who innovates will have for his enemies all those who are well off
under the existing order to things, and only lukewarm supporters in
those who might be better off under the new.

This lukewarm temper arises partly from the fear of adversaries who
have the laws on their side, and partly from the incredulity of mankind,
who will never admit the merit of anything new, until they have seen it
proved by the event. The result, however, is that when the enemies of
change make an attack, they do so with all the zeal of partisans, while the
others defend themselves so feebly as to endanger both themselves and
their cause.

CONCLUSION

In a nutshell, applied strategic thinking has the following characteristics:

1. **Practical:** It is a thought process that can be applied to any job and can be used to examine your role and projects with the goal of becoming better equipped in the future to deliver exceptional results. Applied strategic thinking is not designed for exclusive use by senior leaders or for the annual corporate planning event. However, applied strategic thinking should help support and be aligned with "grand" corporate strategy.

2. **Personalized:** You can and should think like a business. In fact, you are a business, albeit small. If you are to maintain a competitive edge, you must personally take responsibility to adapt to the future, bring maximum value to your function, and outperform others who occupy similar positions in competing organizations. Remember, the timeline or size of the strategic task is irrelevant; the key is that you are thinking ahead (even a little bit helps).

3. **Simple:** Strategy at a personal level doesn't have to be a complex, daunting exercise. A few principles and concepts can be kept in mind and be used collectively or individually. We are not talking about a huge formal process, although there are some helpful tools and a road map to help you put the process down on paper. In reality, many strategic thoughts that enter your mind will be unexpected, sudden, and very natural as you begin to tune into the whole idea and discover that strategy is for you as well as for corporations, the military, or the government.

4. **Future Focused:** It seems like nearly everything you do is evaluated on immediate results or payoff. With applied strategic thinking, you are concerned with getting better positioned to deliver outstanding results in the future. The future is a very relative concept; so strategic thinking can be focused on the next week or next year, such as the next step of a project, your next personal development move, or your preparation to take advantage of new technology coming your way.

5. Aligned: Even though applied strategic thinking is very grass roots, it can and should be aligned with strategy coming down from the top. If strategy isn't being formulated at the top, it is even more important that you attempt to establish some direction and put some strategic targets in your sights so you are not caught off guard by disruptive forces that can threaten corporations as well as individuals.

6. Emerging: Applied strategic thinking is simply figuring out what you need to do before you need to do it. This means you stay alert for incoming information and signals to help you anticipate. Strategic thinking at any level means being an active agent in the way the future unfolds and not sitting back until the future hits you between the eyes. It usually doesn't come as a big bold stroke of genius; it often emerges very incrementally and very intuitively. You need to tune into the data and intuition when it hits, and then muster the courage to take pre-emptive action before it seems obvious or logical to others. If you wait until you have no choice about your course of action, you have not seized the opportunity to be proactive.

> "The way to achieve success is first to have a definite, clear, practical ideal – a goal, an objective. Second, have the necessary means to achieve your ends – wisdom, money, materials, and methods. Third, adjust all your means to that end."
>
> *Aristotle*
> *Greek Philosopher*
> *and Scientist*

In essence, applied strategic thinking will help you search for future solutions that are more productive and enjoyable.

Think about the possibilities. Think about a whole army of people being more strategic, not just the generals. Imagine the possibilities if everyone in your organization devoted a little extra discretionary effort and thought to the future, to how to achieve the future he or she needs and wants. Simply put, solutions for the future won't come easily, par-

ticularly in today's climate. But you can't find
these solutions unless you start looking. If you
could create an army of individuals who have
some concern about future value creation, you
could do immense good for your organization, your customers,
and your use of resources. People in your organization can't be
psychologically punching the clock any more. You have to engage
their hearts, bodies, and minds.

> "Good organizations are living bodies that grow new
> muscles to meet challenges. A[n organization] chart
> demoralizes people. Nobody thinks of himself below
> other people. And in a good company, he isn't."
>
> *Robert Townsend*
> *American Business Writer*

The Fine Art of Practical Strategic Thinking

An Overview

3

An Overview of the Fine Art of Practical Strategic Thinking

The future belongs to those who prepare for it, and luck is merely the residue of preparation. Good fortune and unexpected opportunities are always appreciated gifts; but sustained, long-term success has to be cultivated and developed.

THE SKILLS

Cultivating success means thinking ahead and involves seven essential strategic skill sets, which are the centerpiece of this book. Before we delve into each skill in depth, a preview of these essential skills will provide you with an overview of the complete process of thinking and being more strategic. The chapters that follow will focus on each skill in much more detail.

These seven skills can be used separately (as stand-alone skills), or you can link them together and create a top-to-bottom process. You may encounter situations where some of the strategic thinking has already been done; in these cases, the strategic thinking process is a good review and check-off system or a decision-making filter. You may find that these ideas help in selective situations or on important projects or initiatives that are already underway. So, whether you use these skills systematically or individually, you are likely to develop some thought provoking ideas that will save you some agony, money, and time, as well as increase your contribution to the success of your organization. If you find something intriguing in this chapter, you can jump ahead immediately to the corresponding chapter to acquire more details and insights. Remember, it is never too late to begin acting strategically. Now is the time to reflect on your current situation and prepare for the future. Finally, don't try to do everything at once. Practice a "little learn" from your successes and failures as you develop your "strategic thinking skills." Some consistency and discipline on your part will create discipline for the beast.

1. Tame the Beast

As we alluded to earlier, the first step of the strategic thinking journey centers on a little space creating in your life—creating time to reflect and clearing your head. Extra time and a clear head won't come looking for you. You have to be deliberate as you cre-ate space in your operating world (Zone I). It is not that this zone is bad in and of itself. It is simply that we allow it to get out of control. In fact, many of us have learned to love the frenzied beast. Unless we take deliberate measures to control our daily pressures and grind, our hard work evolves into our worst enemy from a strategic point of view. The 800 pound gorilla can be different for each of us. For some people, the sheer volume of work prevents them from looking ahead. For others, the drama of regular emergencies holds them captive. Some of you may treat everyone else's urgent requests as your own and don't put things into proper perspective. Regardless of the cause, the beast is always close by. If we  manage it well, it can be valuable and even become an ally; if we allow it to run rampant and undisciplined, it can lead to our eventual downfall.

Unfortunately, too many people measure us by how many gorillas we can carry on our backs. Sometimes we mistakenly think that the way to build respect and credibility is to run with the beast and become a pack mule or an extra pair of hands. The key in this step is to take responsibility for the proper care

and feeding of your gorillas. So, how do you get a
leash on the beast?

First, you need to define some strategic ground
rules. Then have the courage and discipline to stick
with them. That means if you need thirty minutes to
think about the week ahead, don't jump into the first skirmish
that comes up. If you need a long lunch each month to plan ahead,
don't compromise it at the first urgent request. Secondly, you have
to block off some time. It doesn't have to be
much, just enough to get your mind in gear.
Thirdly, you must be observant. Take things
in, be curious, ask questions, find out where
your organization is going and link your strategy to it. Fourth, be willing to learn, try the
strategic thinking tools, and trust the process.
Fifth, be ready for some push back and sur-
prised looks. People who aren't accustomed to seeing you in a
strategic light will have to get used to the new you. Anyone can
quibble with your thoughts, analysis, and forecast. Expect some
resistance as natural as you become a strategic change agent or
catalyst.

> **Check Off List**
> 1. Make rules
> 2. Take time
> 3. Observe
> 4. Learn
> 5. Trust in decision

2. Acquire the Target

In order to be a strategic thinker, you must be able to turn off
the operational adrenaline, slow down, and let your mind step
back from the excitement of the action. You
need what we call a strategic dashboard to
help you check out the things that are driving your current success and understand exactly what will drive your future success.

Taking the time to survey your work and
define your priority objectives isn't too difficult; you just need to muster the discipline to
look at your world from a distance and from

> "You just need to
> muster the disci-
> pline to look at
> your world from a
> distance and
> from a different
> perspective."

a different perspective. You may feel this is unproductive – that you won't accomplish anything. And for the truly activity-addicted person, that feeling is normal and natural. In fact you may need a coach, mentor, or associate to provide support along the way to help in managing your 800 pound gorilla. Other people are simply afraid of what they may discover as they unearth their strategic objectives. They may see a lot of strategic holes in their current plan of action. Naturally, this feels very uncomfortable. The key is to assess what you have, where you are (current state), and where you are going (future state or "the point on the horizon"). Then, launch a strategic initiative to establish a strategic position or achieve the "point." No one has enough energy, resources, and emotional capacity to deal with every strategic opportunity or point on the horizon. You must know where to concentrate your effort and be able to make good tradeoffs in order to reach your destination.

> "There is nothing to fear except the persistent refusal to find out the truth, the persistent refusal to analyze the causes of happenings."
>
> *Dorothy Thompson*
> *Journalist and*
> *Anthologist*

In reality, you will have better luck in life if you can get your bearings and discover how to maximize the investment of your time, energy, and resources to create your unique strategic advantage. To do this, you need to pay attention to your personal "strategic dashboard," outlined below.

Your strategic dashboard consists of seven basic elements:

1. Customers – To whom do you pass your product or output on? Who are the people or group of people that use what you produce?

2. People – What is occurring in your relationships with others who have influence and knowledge? Who will be affected by your strategic aims?

3. Products – What are the deliverables or outputs you create? This could be a tangible product or service of any kind.

4. Resources – What do you have to work with (inputs)? Here you need to focus on tangible and physical objects (tools, equipment, funding, time).

5. Processes – What are the distinctive activities, practices, procedures, mechanisms, and methods you use to produce results?

6. You – What is going on with you personally (heart, mind, and body), and what results or position do you want to achieve?

7. Sponsors/Stakeholders – Who is investing in your operation? What are the expected economic returns and results?

If you think your dashboard is a little bit different, then adjust these dashboard areas to fit your particular job, career, profession, or situation. The dashboard is a good place to begin a proactive scan to get a pulse on your situation so you can identify one strategic target to focus on. Going after the future is like going on safari. Wise hunters survey the field before they try to put a target in their sights. Practical strategic thinking is all about hunting for and creating your future before it gets here. No matter what the future holds, you might as well grab it by the horns and steer it as much as possible.

> "Wise hunters survey the field before they try to put a target in their sights."

Undoubtedly there may be many ways to slice and dice your strategic terrain. Don't hesitate to add other strategic gauges to

your dashboard. The idea is to break your world down into manageable pieces. Once you have a compartmentalized picture of your work and key responsibilities, you can begin to size up each area to identify what is going on, what forces are at play, what changes are happening, and what you need to be doing differently in the future.

A thorough survey of the dashboard should help you identify a strategic area of interest (target) that you can act on. You can then begin to close in on the target and achieve the position you ultimately want. Remember to choose your target wisely, because you can't do everything. Pick only a few areas that provide potential for sustained success in the future. And remember strategic thinkers know how to "stay on target."

> "Remember to choose your target wisely, because you can't do everything."

3. Gather Intelligence

Once you have selected a strategic target or position, it is time to gather effective intelligence, interpret the data, and make connections between the data and the strategic target. Although gathering data is one of the most important skills of strategic thinking, it is not a one-time event. By using your own powers of observation and common sense, you can develop an active "antenna" that helps you identify, gather, perceive, and make sense of what is changing in the outside world. Information about the environment is usually plentiful, but it just doesn't get enough attention. Sometimes you have so much going on around you, so much "activity overload," that you pull in the antenna and shut down your thinking. However, in order to lead strategically, you need good intelligence. You need to keep your "ear to the ground."

You not only need good sources of data, but you also need to be a good receiver. You need to be willing to explore, interpret, and draw conclusions from the signals around you. This means making the connections and piecing the data together (a more intense kind of thinking). As you put what you see into a pattern that has meaning, you can begin to detect emerging trends and make associations regarding how things operate and what causes what to happen. For instance, you might see a minor notice online that announces some joint marketing efforts between two of your competitors. You might hear from people in the field about some increased activity or visibility by these competitors. You might learn of a special event that they're co-sponsoring. By themselves, each action might not be overly interesting or alarming. However, when you look at the pattern and see the connection between these activities, they might suggest a concerted and deliberate effort by your competitors to lure your customers away.

> "It is better to be prepared for an opportunity and not have one than to have an opportunity and not be prepared."
>
> *Whitney M. Young Jr.*
> *American social*
> *reformer*

Again, the key is to take the divergent data and information and pinpoint important trends and developments that are relevant to you and your strategic target. Data may provide a strategic signal for you to apply your resources in a special way to protect your position. Likewise, if your intelligence gathering suggests that the competition has dropped the ball and that there is unrest or turmoil within those organizations, it could represent a golden opportunity to launch your own "offensive" strategic move to get a leg up on the competition. As you combine and connect information from the environment, you can compare it with what you know from previous experience and education to see how it all fits together. We are not talking about pure guesswork, because a good part of the future is created from what already exists.

Be open-minded enough to detect the anomalies that may suggest an opportunity or the need for change; consider opposing points of view. This requires a degree of mental flexibility on your part. The goal is to avoid becoming too rigid in your thinking so that you can see new data, come to new conclusions, and create new ways of looking at information to help guide you into the future.

As you develop the capacity to think strategically, you will make more significant contributions to your organization. As you become able to identify leading indicators, accurately forecast future trends and possibilities, and prepare adequately for future eventualities, you will multiply your value. Leaders needn't be oracles or prophets – just insightful, forward-looking, and slightly ahead of the curve. Front-line leaders don't need to anticipate and predict the entire war campaign – just thoughtfully prepare for the important battles where they can make a decisive difference with some preparation and ingenuity. Most of you won't be asked to strategize on high-level corporate direction for the next five years. There is a need, however, for leaders at every level to develop strategic-thinking capability in order to accurately observe, understand, and predict what is going on in their sphere of influence and to contribute to and align with the organization's long-term strategy. Organizations today need people who are futuristic thinkers, not professional futurists. If you want to enhance your performance, you need to recognize that you have your own individual strategic stage to think about.

> "If you want to enhance your performance, you need to recognize that you have your own individual strategic stage to think about."

4. Analyze the Forces

Now that you have identified a worthy target to pursue and have gathered intelligence and information about the target, you are ready to begin applying and working with the data. Begin by analyzing the positive and negative features of the environment surrounding your target or strategic objective. Opposing forces are associated with every strategic target worthy of your effort. You must not put your proverbial head in the sand and ignore these forces. In fact, your intelligence is about to play a big role in helping identify potential threats and opportunities that may open up to you.

The first thing you will need to do is pin-point genuine external forces that could disrupt or help you on your strategic journey. Threats or risks are potential adverse conditions lurking in the environment. They can come from competitors and opponents, weather, equipment, competing priorities, or some other external thing that can sabotage your strategic initiatives' success. Opportunities, on the other hand, are conditions that support and work in your behalf. Everyone experiences good fortune from time to time. Strategic thinkers are able to harness the tail winds to move more quickly.

"Threats are potential adverse conditions lurking in the environment. Opportunities are conditions that support and work in your behalf."

As you evaluate the nature of the threats or opportunities, probe and ask these questions: How big are they? How likely are they? Are they important and serious or just something to be aware of? Then begin thinking about how you could respond to serious threats and how to develop, leverage, and maximize key opportunities. This process involves determining the impact that the opportunity or threat may have on your strategic endeavors and weighing your chances of success.

Taking advantage of opportunities and avoiding threats is not dumb luck. However, you can be totally taken back by unexpected fortune and unpredictable turn of events that no one could have predicted. But most of what happens to you, whether good or bad, can be foreseen if you will develop the skills and discipline to look up, look out, and look around.

After pinpointing and evaluating external threats and opportunities, you need to decide what you are going to do about the likely "high-impact" threats. This analysis will feed directly into the "Chart a Course" step of the strategic thinking process. You must begin to formulate contingency plans now, in case the threat materializes. In other words, if a fire breaks out, what do you do to combat it? How do you react, escape from it, or minimize the impact? However, you must also consider proactive measures in addition to reactive measures. These are the things you can do now to prevent the threat from happening in the first place. You know what they say – "an ounce of prevention is worth a pound of cure." The key at this stage is to define the threats and options. You don't need to initiate action just yet.

Similarly, you must see and prepare to take full advantage of opportunities the environment is making available to you. There may be no such thing as a pure advantage; however, you can actively shape external events, cultivate advantages, and pull out the silver lining even from a catastrophe. Someone once said that the harder you work, the luckier you get; maximizing opportunities is not a passive activity. Another old adage says, "Luck favors a prepared mind." You can't sit around waiting for fortune to hit you in the head. You have to be an active force to help nurture and leverage opportunities.

Like outside threats, opportunities need to be identified from the intelligence that you have investigated, evaluated, and highlighted. Good strategic thinkers are threat – and opportunity – hunters. They are selective; they go after the good stuff while making plans to deal with the rest.

Unlike threats and opportunities, which are external in nature, strengths and limitations exist now, in real time; and they are internal and controllable in nature. They represent who you are and are within your control. You have more influence over your strengths and

"Very often we are our own worst enemy as we foolishly build stumbling blocks on the path that leads to success and happiness."

Louis Binstock
American Reform
Rabbi

limitations than you do over external circumstances that serve up both threats and opportunities.

The challenge is that it is easy to overlook assets, talents, experience, and resources that you have accumulated and that can be applied to your strategic journey. Likewise, it is easy to deny, rationalize, or underestimate limitations. Skipping this honest, introspective work is a huge mistake. A realistic assessment of what it is that you bring or don't bring to the party is vital.

Reflective assessment about strengths and limitations can help you inventory how you (and the immediate world you control) can be an ally or an obstacle. Once you journey inward, you can move to the next task of developing scenarios and putting the actual game plan together. A strengths and limitations as-sessment doesn't have to be complex. You just need to gather a variety of perspectives and opinions, quantify the importance and value of each strength or weakness as it relates to the target, and formulate countermeasures and actions to offset limitations while maximizing your strengths.

The key to this phase of strategic thinking is awareness. No one can be strong in every area. But if you have an accurate picture, you can choose smart tradeoffs and proceed with confidence

> "Analyzing what you haven't got as well as what you have is a necessary ingredient of a career."
>
> *Orison Swett*
> *Marden*
> *American Author*

and full knowledge of your capacity to act, while being aware that you may be vulnerable in some areas. Strengths fortify you against outside threats, and limitations expose you even more to outside threats. Strengths can help you exploit opportunities, and your limitations can hamper your ability to take full advantage of these opportunities. Knowing what specific tools you have available in your arsenal will help you wage a strategic battle more effectively. Again, you will be in a better position to figure out if you are well-suited to pursue your target once you consider the external forces and the internal resources. Remember, you need a good match between your target and your strengths; strategic actions move in concert with your strengths and limitations.

5. Define Scenarios

Your effectiveness as a strategic thinker is largely dependent on your ability to predict how events will likely turn out in the future. Good leaders have the capacity to describe end results or effects based on their assessment of the intelligence, external forces, and internal resources. In some circumstances, you might choose to act decisively; in other situations, you might observe conditions, bide your time, and tread water for a while. You might see an opportunity to influence the direction of events, and then conclude that the timing isn't right or that there won't be a direct impact or desired results if you act now.

This awareness will help you determine whether you should deploy your assets, try to control or influence the environment, or take a more protective stance against things that are difficult to control. Strategic thinkers are rational and realistic; they work within their

> "If I had eight hours to chop down a tree, I'd spend six hours sharpening my ax."
> *Abraham Lincoln*

circle of control and influence. This places them in a proactive stance and prevents them from being "blind-sided," becoming victims of circumstance, or engaging in un-winnable battles. When the likely scenario doesn't look good you have to be willing to trim your sails, back off, and look at another target.

The construction of scenarios is like making a blueprint or mental picture. Envision yourself as an architect with a picture in your mind of a likely positive outcome. Then construct a picture of a likely negative scenario where you anticipate an unfavorable outcome. Use your experience, knowledge, and creativity to scope out the scenarios in detail.

But you can't limit yourself to just these two obvious, likely scenarios. Thoroughly building scenarios requires a comprehensive examination of a unique third possible outcome: the "alternative scenario," which may be unusual or a surprise outcome or eventuality. This is when you have to get out of your box, dig deeper, and get creative about your theory of how the future will unfold and what it will be like down the road.

With any project, an architect doesn't begin the plan without checking the accuracy of his or her data and reviewing the information with others. Similarly, effective strategic thinkers confirm, check, and adjust their blueprints to ensure accuracy before moving forward. It is too easy to put the cart before the horse, to do a classic "ready" – "fire" – (OOPS) "aim," or worse "fire," "ready," "aim" approach.

> "Every well built house started in the form of a definite purpose plus a definite plan in the nature of a set of blueprints."
>
> *Napoleon Hill*
> *American Author*

So before you launch yourself on a strategic journey, you need to envision the potential outcomes.

You are now at a key decision point because you are one step closer to "serious action." You need to decide whether to keep moving forward or to step back and evaluate your strategic **idea, decision** or **action** (I.D.A.). If you are not comfortable with the scenarios, you may be looking at a "no go" I.D.A. situation. It all comes down to judgment and common sense. Keep in mind that you are looking at the future, so there are some unknowns, and you will have to make some intelligent judgment calls here. Rely on your instincts and experience to help you decide to press forward with your I.D.A. and scope out a concrete course of action.

6. Chart a Course

There is never a perfect course of action. Every plan should be constructed with the thought in mind that you will have to adjust it. The plan should take full advantage of the intelligence-gathering mechanism, reflect the threats and opportunities, and factor in capabilities and limitations that will impact your strategic target and the moves you need to begin making now. Additionally, you will need to incorporate your "shopping list" of requirements needed to execute your plan of action. The course of action is a set of specific actions that can be assigned and tracked. The plan is a road-map and a pathway forward. The course of action represents a distillation of all of the strategic thinking phases. In short, the course of action is the bridge between thinking and execution.

Your course of action or game plan is a detailed roadmap of who will do what, where, when, and how (a lot of sub-plans). A clearly defined plan keeps people aligned and informed. It eliminates chaos and confusion. Some people are natural planners, whereas others have to be very deliberate and consciously lay out a plan of action on paper. Regardless of the formality or informality of your plan, you and your team need to know the assignments, actions, due dates, and expectations regarding when and how things will get done. The plan defines and integrates the method, means, time, and place. It can start with what you might do, or what you should do, and end with what you will do. As you design your plan, be creative, brainstorm different routes, and incorporate contingency plans. Charting a course will specifically define "how" the target is to be acquired and achieved. Armed with a good plan, the troops will be ready to roll out and hit some targets.

> "The plan defines and integrates the method, means, time, and place."

7. Mobilize and Sustain

Without action, strategic thinking is reduced to mental gymnastics. There are four key ingredients to effective action:

1. Courage
2. Speed
3. Concentration
4. Sustainability

> "It is not always what we know or analyzed before we make a decision that makes it a great decision. It is what we do after we make the decision to implement and execute it that makes it a good decision."
>
> *William Pollard*
> *Chairman and CEO*
> *of ServiceMaster Co.*

These four principles allow you to hit the target hard, which, after all, is what it is all about – RESULTS.

Great strategic thinkers gain advantage when they act courageously. Naturally, when you commit your resources and energy, carrying out the plan can be a bit daunting. It is easy to second-guess or doubt the wisdom of your actions. You may fight two urges: one is to attack, and the other is to fall back and be cautious. Caution is a great thing in the right situation. However, when you have made the preparations, completed the calculations, and determined that the conditions are ripe for success, it is time to jump in with both feet, make a splash, and move out quickly. You can't execute if you are faint of heart. Strategic execution requires a leap of faith. Intelligence will never be perfect; the future cannot be absolutely known. You have to be fearless at this stage. Action has to co-exist with your concerns. You probably won't win every time because nobody is perfect, but your "batting average" will be higher with a bit of strategic thinking.

Again, at this stage of the process, it is time to act. So be clear about what you should do right now. The journey of a thousand miles begins with the first step. You have evaluated your options, prepared your plans, you see the risks, now you are ready to push on despite any fears. This is called determination.

> **Remember:** When you launch a
> strategy, the greatest limitation
> you face may be self-imposed
> fear and hesitation.

Now be prepared to accelerate. You must put all the horsepower to work and ignite your engines. You have done a thorough up-front analysis. You have been patient and careful, so now is the time to sprint and gain the high ground. Those who move at a snail's pace make themselves vulnerable to threats and barriers. The advantage goes to those who can execute strategic actions early and quickly. Those who are both fearless and nimble are a formidable force.

Concentration means focusing your assets and capabilities and releasing them at the right time with as much force as possible. Don't try to do everything all at once and allow yourself to get spread too thin. You don't want to overextend and be overcommitted. You may need stages and phases for your offensive move. The number one objective is to secure some wins! Control your aspirations by setting your sights and matching your appetite with your resources. Military leaders, for example, have learned with great suffering and enormous costs what can happen when they have to fight too many fronts and whose offensive force was spread too thin and too long.

> "Success is not final, failure is not fatal: it is the courage to continue that counts."
> *Winston Churchill*

Finally, leaders must finish what they start. Ineffective action and lack of follow-through are the source of so much waste in organizations. Decide now what actions will best support the programs and changes you introduce. Every new effort will face direct and indirect resistance. Many initiatives are met with excitement that wears off quickly. Reinforce and maintain your progress and momentum. The key is not to start something that you don't plan to – or are unable to – sustain. Strategic initiatives need to be nurtured and maintained if you want them to bear fruit. You will have to exercise a great deal of discipline to achieve strategic success.

CONCLUSION

We have discovered that great strategic thinkers in any position or at any level of an organization know how to apply these skills. They avoid succumbing to and being seduced by the activity addiction. Good strategic thinkers develop their skills by practicing and hunting "small game" (projects, assignments, and team issues) first. Later they may assume key corporate positions or become political leaders or military strategists on a much larger scale.

Most of you probably won't be world leaders or generals. But all of you will fulfill valuable roles in organizations. Your contribution will increase if you master the principles and skills of personal strategic thinking. They are skills that can be learned or acquired with just a little commitment and desire. Yes, there will be some formidable forces to overcome. You will have to be less enslaved by your own comfortable thought patterns and your traditional views and solutions to problems. You will have to develop patience and move away from the "task magnet" (operational beast) to give your mind a chance to breathe, think, reflect, and contemplate. You will have to resist constant pressure for instant results, quick fixes, and fast solutions to every challenge or dilemma. In short, you will have to be courageous and bold as you try to bring more balance and a strategic perspective into your life.

> "You just don't luck into things as much as you'd like to think you do. You build step by step, whether it's friendships or opportunities."
>
> *Barbara Bush*
> *American First Lady*

The journey won't necessarily be simple or easy. It will take an investment in training and practice. But the journey will be worth it. You can be more successful if you think ahead, determining what it will take to make a difference and make a greater contribution. You can avoid a lot of heartache when you anticipate forces that can lift you up or take you down. When you adopt

 an innovative and proactive mindset, you will be more prepared for the tough decisions, realities, and opportunities that come your way. You can prepare your team to weather the storms and to move out when the sun appears.

> "Visualize this thing that you want, see it, feel it, believe in it. Make your mental blue print, and begin to build."
>
> *Robert Collier*
> *American Author*

Experiment with these ideas, and add liberally to these fundamental skills and ideas as you steer your ship into the future. We are convinced the strategic process will change your life in positive ways with a little thought, some heart, discipline, and a lot of determined action.

> "The future is not a result of choices among alternative paths offered by the present, but a place that is created; created first in mind, then in will and next in activity. The future is not someplace we are going to, but one we are creating. The paths to it are not found but made and the activity of making them changes the maker and the destination."
>
> *John Scharr*

CHAPTER FOUR

Tame the Beast

4

Tame the Beast

As we indicated in the Strategic Landscape chapter, becoming a more strategic person requires a certain amount of discipline and determination in order to manage 800 pound gorillas we all carry on our backs. From our research, the biggest challenge that you will face as a strategic person is being able to concentrate on the future and to find unique, breakthrough ideas that will help you add additional value to your organization. The problem is finding the time, energy, discipline, and skill to break loose from the routine "activity magnet." If you can't find some "calm" in your life, you won't find your strategic direction.

Society seems so caught up in the "win today" mentality that few of us are able to escape from the pressure of the beast to deliver results now. The value of shaping the future isn't appreciated in some circles. Our world places a great deal of value on tactical efficiency, often at the expense of future success. The fact is that all of us have conspired to create what we affectionately call the "operational beast." Sometimes the culture of the organization produces the beast and pressures you to react rather than create. Other times your own comfort level with the familiar or the perceived security of the status quo creates the trap, allowing the beast to swallow you. Becoming more strategic is a lot like a rocket trying to blast off to escape the earth's gravitational pull. It takes a lot of force to break away, but once you have, you are able to see a whole new perspec-

> "Becoming more strategic is a lot like a rocket trying to blast off to escape the earth's gravitational pull."

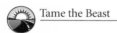

tive on your world. When this happens, it is truly refreshing and liberating. As we said earlier, we are not suggesting that you should always keep your head in the clouds, become less efficient, or be a poor executor or tactician. We just believe that there should be some room in your life to think long term, to step away from the heat of the action, and to look for new or better things that will produce success tomorrow.

In order to move into a more strategic frame of mind, you need to determine how powerful the beast is, what is driving it, and how stuck you are. To be great at what you do, you have to be good at being expedient and efficient with your operational responsibilities, while also being good at innovating and figuring out ways to be distinctive and proactive in the future. The following poem by Charles Osgood, a well known television broadcaster, summarizes our thoughts about the beast of complacency:

Pretty Good

There once was a pretty good student, who sat in a pretty good class.
And was taught by a pretty good teacher, who always let pretty good pass.

He wasn't terrific at reading, he wasn't a whiz-bang at math,
But for him education was leading, straight down a pretty good path.

He didn't find school too exciting, but he wanted to do pretty well,
And he did have some trouble with writing, and nobody had taught him to spell.

When doing arithmetic problems, pretty good was regarded as fine.
Five plus five needn't always add up to be 10, a pretty good answer was 9.

The pretty good class that he sat in, was part of a pretty good school.
And the student was not an exception, on the contrary, he was the rule.

The pretty good student in fact was part of a pretty good mob.
And the first time he knew what he lacked, was when he looked for a pretty good job.

It was then, when he sought a position, he discovered that life could be tough.
And he soon had a sneaky suspicion, pretty good, might not be good enough.

The pretty good town in our story was part of a pretty good state.
Which had pretty good aspirations, and prayed for a pretty good fate.

There once was a pretty good nation, pretty proud of the greatness it had,
Which learned much too late, if you want to be great,

Pretty good, is in fact pretty bad.

Again, it is important for you to not only be pretty good at your tactical responsibilities, but also at how you can mold and shape a great long-term future for your team, your organization, and yourself.

Our experience and findings suggest that the following factors combine to make it difficult for you to escape the grip of the beast.

Factor #1: Complacency

You can easily be lulled into complacency by the routine aspects of your work. It is like your mind goes onto auto pilot. You get seduced into thinking that you are getting something done when in truth, you are just going through the motions. Actually, some people are very good at going through the motions rather than reinventing the motions that will pave a way to future success. You may have even learned to make the motions fun, making it difficult to break the monotony and the endless cycle that you are in. Some people feel enslaved by their mind-numbing routines, while other people don't mind them because they have never been encouraged or rewarded for thinking ahead and out of the box. In fact, they may have not ever seen the outside of the box. Don't settle for or accept complacency. Challenge yourself and pursue something beyond the routine. Establish the discipline to pause and ask yourself tough questions: Are you ready for the future? Are you getting the results that are really important? Are you doing anything to free up your thinking?

Factor #2: Difficulties

You may become very impatient when you encounter difficulties or struggles with your day-to-day work. You may respond to these situations with knee-jerk reactions and quick fixes, lacking the discipline to think deeply and explore new possibilities.

Avoid being caught up with over analyzing causes and diagnosing why things are going wrong. Spend a little time thinking about new approaches that will lead to a different and more productive future. When you find yourself facing a repetitive tactical problem or difficult situation, before responding, look at it as an opportunity to break off from the present and let your mind move to a higher strategic look at the situation.

Factor #3: Fire Fighting

The pressures and stress of many jobs today soak up so much concentration and effort that finding the energy to step back from the rapid-fire action in order to plan ahead and prepare for the future becomes difficult. When you have to juggle many stressful situations during the course of a day, everything begins to look like a crisis or emergency.

We understand people in organizations need to be good fire fighters and emergency technicians. Yet, many find rescue work and performing heroic deeds very rewarding. Sometimes the action and excitement become addicting, energizing, and fun. Becoming more strategic is not an easy mental transition given the fact that so much emphasis, reinforcement, and attention get placed on a crisis response mode of operation. All of this combined makes it difficult to look to the future. Avoid succumbing to these forces and feelings. Give yourself permission to turn your attention away from the "blazes." We once heard someone say, when you find yourself captivated by the daily sunset (or your tactical responsibilities), turn around and discover the beauty in the other direction. It really works! Deliberately moving in the opposite direction of the daily pull can produce fresh insights.

"Give yourself permission to turn your attention away from the 'blaze.'"

Factor #4: Environment

Organization norms, values, or even upper management may discourage you from thinking ahead; or you may feel exposed and in the spotlight too much if you spend time in the strategic zone. We regularly find that people in organizations are told "thinking ahead is the job of the people higher up." In addition, you may receive a lot of short-term recognition from management when you are able to heroically save the day or execute the laundry list of activities, even though the activities may be meaningless in the long-term scheme of things. After all, who gets recognized for predicting, anticipating, or thinking ahead before any real payoff is in place? It takes personal resolve and dedication to withstand the initial questioning, second guessing, and even ridicule when you try to think ahead, "see around corners," as Colin Powell calls it, and get positioned to harness change.

Factor #5: "Wing it"

Some people are naturally spontaneous; they are able to "wing it." Some people even wing it very well. They are talented and can "fly by the seat of their pants." They have rarely needed to antici- 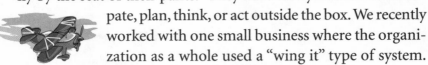 pate, plan, think, or act outside the box. We recently worked with one small business where the organization as a whole used a "wing it" type of system. They had been very successful, and this mode of operation seemed to be working for them on the surface. But as they grew and the demand for their service increased, they soon discovered that winging it would not work for the future. We were pleased when they were finally able to look forward and predict the future and figured out how to adapt and shape it. However, the challenge they faced was breaking away from their traditional routine ways of responding and forcing themselves to think ahead. The lure of falling back on their old modes of operating was amazingly powerful. But with rigorous discipline, focused efforts, and even a little self-development training, they were able to begin resisting the temptation to "fly by the seat of their pants." Falling back into the trap is easy; so even today, they are continuously working towards fundamentally changing their business.

"Escaping the Beast"

So, what is the solution to these obstacles and barriers? The good news is that they can be overcome; the bad news is that it takes some work. If it were easy, everyone would be more strategic. The fact is that it does require work and discipline to create the opportunity for you to differentiate yourself from other people or functions that have been consumed by the "operational beast."

Again, we want to stress that being strategic doesn't mean that you stop doing the things that must get done each day. It does require that you find a way to mentally step back and have a conversation about the future with yourself or with a mentor, team member, or trusted advisor. The key is to give your mind a chance to breathe a little, to step out of the daily tactics and automatic maneuvers. One important step you can take is to learn how the organization and its parts fit together; try to see the big picture. To do this means you have to be open to becoming a generalist, as well as a specialist, working in a narrow field. You have to be curious and willing to take some risks, explore different things, and talk to different people, as well as try different jobs, build networks, and find out what makes your organization tick. You may want to visit a customer (internal or external) or attend a workshop.

> "You have to be curious and willing to take some risks."

Second, you have to develop the spirit of curiosity and discovery. You have to look for ways and means of taking some risks and experimenting. We are not talking about crazy, poorly calculated risks; we are talking about those moments when you can explore and test ideas out. Arrange for some solo time where you can isolate yourself, without distractions and interruptions, so you can think about how to better position your work and achieve outstanding results. Develop habits and skills that will strengthen a strategic mind:

- Be curious
- Be self-motivated
- Be reflective and dream
- Be playful with ideas
- Be collaborative
- Be flexible
- Seek out knowledge and information
- Observe and study others who operate strategically
- Find a mentor who helps you think and who asks tough questions
- Go on a learning journey

As you begin to get into a strategic mode, don't let your mind wander back to the operational activity trap too quickly.

Third, you need to increase your capacity and defer some immediate rewards in exchange for longer term benefits. It is all about making good tradeoffs, investing some of your time, resources, and talents in long term opportunities, and preparing for future rainy days. Think of it as a financial Certificate of Deposit (CD) in which you put your savings. Your funds are tied up for a period of time, but once a certain amount of time passes, you have a significant return on your investment.

Fourth, you have to learn to be flexible and adaptable to

changes coming your way. People who remain rigid and inflexible get stuck in the status quo and are unable to go with the flow. So don't get uptight when the winds of change blow your way. Dig deep and discover the silver lining in change and apparent adversity. Sometimes it takes courage to challenge conventional ways of doing things, but that is what a strategic  person is able to do. You must be able to shake things up a bit. Let your mind go to the creative edge and explore radically new or disruptive innovations that people are talking about. Try some occasional bold moves, surprise yourself, and be an active force in the creation of the future that you want to see unfold.

> "Try some occasional bold moves, surprise yourself, and be an active force in the creation of the future that you want to see unfold."

Fifth, you need to find the right environment for you, one that will foster a situation where you can stay clear of the operational beast. Consider these specific factors:

- Time of day (morning, afternoon, or evening)

- Temperature (warm or cool)

- Area (formal or informal, cluttered or clean)

- Noise/stimulus (quiet or active)

- Light (bright or dim, natural or artificial)

- Working area (desk, floor, bench, couch, etc.)

- Seating arrangement (reclined, straight backed, etc.)

- Supplies and resources (notes, laptop computer, etc.)

- Clothing (We heard of one study that indicated people whose feet were comfortable were 11% more creative.)

Applied strategic thinking will help your search for future solutions be more productive, organized, and enjoyable. Creating a circle of individuals concerned with personal value creation could do immense good for your organization, your customers, your resources, and yourself. People in the organization wouldn't be punching the clock any more. They would have their hearts, bodies, and minds engaged in the future possibilities.

> "We cannot all be John Cabots, sailing off into the blue with the king's patent to discover new lands; but we can be explorers in spirit, with democracy's mandate to make this land better by discovering new ways of living and doing things."
>
> "The spirit of exploration, whether it be of the surface of the earth or the principles of living greatly, includes developing the capacity to face trouble with courage, disappointment with cheerfulness, and triumph with humility."
>
> *From the Royal Bank of Canada Newsletter*

CHAPTER FIVE

Acquire the Target

5

Acquire the Target

This may be the most important skill or step along the strategic thinking highway. The last thing you want to do in life is chase red herrings or launch big campaigns before you have a sense of destination or a position you want to achieve. So before you do a ready . . . fire . . . (oops) . . . aim, you will want to create and define what it is you are going after, what matters, and what will make a difference in your future success. We believe in the philosophy that a well defined strategic solution is half executed.

Strategic Target

Simply put, a strategic target is a clearly defined description of what you want to <u>do</u> differently, to <u>have</u> (result), or to <u>be</u> in the future. Fundamentally, it is the position you want to reach or the core change you want to make. We like to call it your I.D.A. (idea, decision, or action). The target must be something worth fighting for, because you perceive it as key to the future success of your group, team, family, or yourself. Your I.D.A. should specify how you intend to shape the future, and it should put the future clearly in the cross hairs of your intentions. The target will help you stay sharp and be more effective in the future. It will also have a huge impact on your resources and personal energy because of the skeptics and the resistance you are likely to encounter.

> "Next in importance to having a good aim is to recognize when to pull the trigger."
>
> *David Letterman*
> *Television Talk Host*

In a nutshell, the target is your strategic intent. Some people can find direction by accident, but for most people it requires disciplined thought. As one of our close friends used to say, "Even a blind squirrel will find a nut once in a while." The point is simple: it is better to fly into the future with your eyes wide open than to stick your head in the sand and hope you snag success by chance.

Select a Target

The first thing to understand about the strategic thinking highway is that you can select a target from many fields of opportunity. To start, look at the big picture and take in the whole landscape that lies before you as you get your bearings, and pick a point to aim for on the horizon. Get a feel for where you are now, for what is working and what isn't. Ask yourself these types of questions first:

> "If you don't know where you are going, how can you expect to get there?"
> *Basil S. Walsh*
> *American Author*

- How would I characterize my current situation overall?

- Am I satisfied with my success and progress?

- What has made me successful?

- How can I repeat success?

- How did I arrive at my current position or situation?

Next, move down a layer in your questioning. Ask yourself questions like these:
- What are my hopes and dreams for the future?

- What is my vision for my work, life, or team?

- What are my broad goals and ambitions?

- What will drive my success in the future?

- Is anything holding me back?

- What are the obstacles?

- What is keeping me from making more progress?

- What is missing in my work or life?

- What do I really want before it is over?

- What am I worried about?

Up to this point, what you have really done is brain-dump to create the big picture. This is a good warm-up. Brainstorm these types of questions before you get more specific in any one I.D.A. (idea, decision or action). Notice what it is that you are paying attention to, what it is that either is appealing or uncomfortable. The thoughts and ideas you put down will create a backdrop or screen against which you can validate the more specific target you are about to create. You can return to your overall assessment of the past, present, and future once you have identified a more specific target.

Be Specific

In the next phase of "acquiring the target," you will move much deeper and become more specific. However, avoid making the big mistake of taking on more than you can chew at one time. You have finite resources and energy to invest in your future I.D.A, so choose wisely, and focus on a few vital initiatives rather than trying to pull off too many at once. If you have a lot of really good targets, prioritize them and do a few well rather than a lot poorly. When you have a target or a point on the horizon, you can begin to focus, organize, and direct your efforts towards it.

Strategic Dashboard

As you drive your automobile down the highway, you periodically check the information on the dashboard: fuel gauge, speedometer, odometer, computer, compass, engine functions, etc. When driving down the strategic thinking highway, you also have a dashboard of variables that contribute to your success. The "Strategic Thinking Dashboard" has seven key areas, and your strategic target will be embedded in one of these seven areas. You will want to explore each of these dimensions to find which one might be a "hot button" for you. Each of these seven "gauges" is critical to your performance in the future. Keep in mind that you could discover multiple strategic targets once you begin to look at each dashboard gauge.

> "If opportunity doesn't knock, build a door."
> *Milton Berle*
> *American Comic*

1. CUSTOMERS

The first area of the strategic thinking dashboard is the CUSTOMERS. By customers, we mean those you serve immediately, people or groups who use what you make or do or who need your help. In some cases, your customers may be the people or groups that follow after you and contribute additional work before the product or service reaches the final customer. Basically, a customer is someone you deliver your work to, the beneficiaries of your service, the end consumer of the product or service, or one who purchases what you do. Other possibilities are an internal customer, a client, a user, or someone who receives your work. Whether you want to admit it or not, you are all in business and you have a clientele. Sometimes clients are powerful, visible, and vocal, and sometimes they are quiet, lacking in power and voice.

It doesn't matter what they are like, they are out there, and they are a dynamic and important strategic force to understand as you think about selecting a target.

You may have many different segments or types of customers. Whoever they are, what is important is that you think about them, define them, and analyze what they want now and in the future. Have you ever thought about how to proactively retain your customer base? Perhaps some of you may say that your customers are "locked in, because if they want maintenance work done on their computer they have to see me—that's company policy." Well, that may be policy now. It may have also been the policy in the past. But it may not be the policy in the future. If your customers are not happy they will go elsewhere, or they will pressure those who manage policy to make a change that may not be in your best interest.

> "A satisfied customer is the best business strategy of all."
>
> *Michael LeBoeuf*
> *Author*

When thinking about your customers, reflect on why your customers come to you: Are they forced to work with you, or do they want to and choose to work with you? What will your customers need in the future? What options and alternatives might your customers have for your product, service, or contribution? These are the thoughts you have to confront in a practical sense, even though your customers seem content right now. This is the time to think about how to remain in a position where you are in demand by your customer. Keep in mind that you may need to look for entirely new products and services for entirely new customers who don't fit within your current business model.

Competition as it relates to an individual person or team is not exactly like a Fortune 500 conglomerate's competition. Your competition may be radically new or disruptive technology, new techniques, or better service from some other source. You have to be one step ahead of this practical and subtle competition, or you will become irrelevant and ultimately out of business! So you must

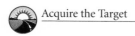

update and innovate, understand your customers and where they are going in the future, and parallel your efforts to be one step ahead in adding value and quietly leading your customers. In short, you have an informal and probably unspoken contract with your customer about current expectations and emerging future expectations that you should strategically be discovering now. Do you understand your "contract" (the expectations) with your customer, or have you defined your "value proposition" as it is sometimes called? A strategic target focused on this dash-

"You have to be one step ahead of this practical and subtle competition, or you will become irrelevant and ultimately out of business!"

 board area is all about understanding why your customers come to you instead of using someone else; what will cause them to stick with you as a preferred solution in the future. Also, consider your customers of the future: who they are and what they may need. They may be entirely different than the group you serve today.

2. PEOPLE

The second dashboard area where you could harvest a strategic target is PEOPLE, your network of allies or partners. Strategic people have a system of relationships that support their success. Allies are people who have a tremendous influence on your suc-

 cess. Too many people don't give their allies enough thought. You run hard in the operational mode from day to day without thinking about your partners and sponsors, those who are quietly working on your behalf. Ironically, you may not even realize what they do for you. It doesn't really matter. The fact is that they are there. Charlie Plumb, a Navy pilot and six year POW from the Vietnam conflict, was shot down during one of his missions. Only when he was confined and had time to

reflect did he realize how important his partners had been to him in the past and were to his survival now. He said he gained a great appreciation for the regular sailors down in the bowels of the ship who folded the silk and prepared his parachute every day. Charlie asks  the question: Do you have any parachute packers, and do you show your appreciation? Or do you wait until you are in dire straits before you acknowledge your parachute packers?

In short, you must examine these questions about your allies:

- Who looks out for you now, and who will in the future?

- Do you have trusted mentors or advisors?

- How can you find more allies, given the type of future you are moving into and the type of future you want to create for yourself?

- How can you best maintain and energize your allies?

- What new alliances can you form?

- What would it take to expand your network?

3. PRODUCTS

The third gauge on the dashboard is the PRODUCTS, service, or contribution itself. Again, you may be thinking what you are actually responsible for producing doesn't really count in the grand scheme of things. This is bad thinking! What you contrib-  ute does count. Certainly, it counts for you and your team. The question is how good it is? In fact, the strategic question is, "Will it be good enough in the future?" You need to insure that your product is value added; that is, it provides a solution to your customer's needs or problems. To be successful long term, products need to be of significant quality and be perceived as valuable to the customer. Strategic thinkers ask themselves:

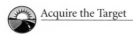

- What advantages do my products or services offer?
- Is my product distinctive, and does it stand out from other choices that are emerging and that the customer will have in the future?
- Are there entirely new things that I can position myself to offer?

Strategic thinkers constantly look for new ways to update, improve, and refine their products or create new services. This means periodically inventing or reinventing the service or product. Strategic thinkers are proactively looking for ways to do it better, smarter, faster, and cheaper. You can't wait until obsolescence catches up with you and forces you to give up your comfort zone. You have to be consistently thinking and experimenting.

> "Strategic thinkers constantly update, improve, and refine their products or create new services."

If your product or output becomes the target area, and you relentlessly search out new solutions or make refinements in your product before they are required or before you get the mandate, you  will inevitably succeed more often. Is there a cost to making adjustments to your products or delivery? Sure! Will your innovations be immediately welcomed by everyone with open arms? Probably not. That is because you are thinking a step ahead of the curve. You are on the leading edge of change. Others probably don't or won't see it until it is too late. This mode of thinking will lead them to being road kill on the strategic interstate!

Changing your products or services, creating new ones, and becoming an inventor of your future requires courage. You have to know what you are willing to trade and to trade off. The past doesn't die easily, but you must systematically kill what you have created if you are to survive and thrive in the future. A change doesn't have to be a total overhaul. You can do it slowly, but you must do it or fall victim to the grim reaper of obsolescence and irrelevance. A little forethought can go a long way in heading off a lot of pain. It was W. Edwards Deming who said, "Plan, do, think, act." A stra-  tegic target focused on your product doesn't always have to be an earth-shattering breakthrough or new technology. It can be testing out a new prototype service, talking to your customers, doing some benchmarking, or investing a portion of your time and resources in piloting, exploring, and offering some new twists to your products that will benefit your customers.

4. RESOURCES

In your search for a priority strategic target, the fourth area to examine is RESOURCES. By resources we mean the inputs required to create your product or service. This could include the raw materials that you need, required equipment, tools, or supplies you use. In some fields of work, resources may be the  intangible things: information, data, people, and reports. In other fields, they are more tangible: supplies, hardware, material, commodities, money, and technology. Strategically you have to ask yourself the following questions:

- What is happening in this part of the dashboard?
- Who are my resource suppliers?
- How good are my sources?
- How are the sources or is the supply chain changing?
- If the concept of my contribution or my services changes how will it affect my resources?
- What will the supply and demand for these resources be in the future?

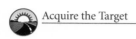

- Will I get enough of what I will need?
- What if the cost of supplies increases or decreases substantially? How will I respond?
- What totally new resources and options are out there?
- Should I shift my personal supply lines in some way?

> "By resources, we mean the inputs required to create your product or service."

In this area of the dashboard, you have to find the balance between diversification and concentration of your resources. You have to think about your level of dependence on certain ingredients. For example, how will you adapt if the price of fuel begins to increase dramatically? What will you do if a key player goes away, a strike hits one of your suppliers, or the government changes the accounting rules on trading bonds or on the regulation of drugs? All of these forces could have a huge impact on your resource base and hence your ability to build a quality product or service to deliver to your internal or external customer. If you are thinking ahead, you won't feel undue stress, you won't be overly surprised, and you will have plan B or C ready to implement at the slightest hint of a change or disruption in your resources. You will be well ahead of the curve as others scramble to figure out what to do or how to replace a vital resource.

Again, the aim is to zero in on the real linchpins necessary for your operation to run smoothly in the future. When you exercise your thinking in terms of a few vital resources or suppliers, it will be much easier and more natural to respond and adapt when there is a change involving resources.

5. PROCESSES

The fifth area to examine in your search for the right strategic target is the area of PROCESSES. Processes symbolize the way  you turn resources into products and services. This means your unique way of working, and how you apply intangible and tangible resources to add distinctive value to your product or service. A process consists of a number of activities that are triggered by other events and that ultimately are transformed into a product or service. Processes are systems, methods, and techniques that you employ to create your products. Clayton Christensen describes it well in his book, *The Innovators Dilemma:* "Processes are simply your patterns of interaction, coordination and decision making. Some processes are formal in the sense that they are explicitly defined, visibly documented, and consciously followed.

> "Processes are systems, methods, and techniques that you employ to create your products."

Often, processes are informal, habitual routines or ways of working that have instinctively evolved over time." As is true for the processes and methods of the big multi-nationals, there are advantages if your unique processes and methods are streamlined and efficient. Once again, the whole key is your ability to develop and gear your process to provide distinctive value in the future. For example, a process could be how you do any of the following things:

- Research and design
- Package and sell
- Ensure quality
- Maintain records and logs
- Make decisions and solve problems
- Budget and manage finances

- Transport and deliver
- Construct and assemble
- Manage customer complaints
- Develop your team
- Make your work simpler or better
- Negotiate with suppliers
- Determine prices
- Administrate
- Customer Service
- Logistics

Many people don't think about their processes very often and get into the trap of blindly doing things the way they have always done it. Changing and letting go of the "how" (traditional processes) can be as difficult as letting go of the "what" (traditional products or services). Processes have to be flexible to adapt to changes in the environment.

When hunting for a personal strategic initiative, it is easy to overlook this area of the dashboard. You may perceive that your routines, habits, and actions are incidental and not central to becoming strategic. But we encourage you to rigorously investigate this area for possible strategic opportunity and not take this area for granted. Do some careful reflection and explore the tough questions:

"Do some careful reflection and explore the tough questions."

- Are your methodologies as efficient as they will need to be to take on the future?

- Are your practices as reliable and consistent as will be necessary to meet future requirements?

- Do the people around you follow and support effective and consistent processes?

- Are the methods and process documented well, defined, and followed with discipline?

- What changes are on the horizon for new protocols and techniques?

- Can new ideas be tried out in your area of responsibility?

- Which processes are the vital ones that glue your world together?

- When was the last time you tried doing it a new way, and how flexible are you?

Fixing something in your processes can help free you up to do more strategic thinking. Perhaps it all starts here.

6. YOU

The sixth dashboard area is YOU. This is certainly not the least important of the target search areas. Too many of you ignore your own personal needs until you are stressed out or burned out. Sometimes you are too humble or too embarrassed to take care of yourself until you jeopardize your  future. You have to be thinking about the capabilities and compe-

> "You need the strength to do battle with the future, and to do this you must develop your skills and sharpen the saw."

tencies needed for future success. Consider, for example, how many times people change jobs or career directions in a lifetime.

Someone that we were close to was a perfect example. As a supervisor on the railroad, he worked excessively long and hard for 35 years. He had a comfortable retirement economically; but unfortunately, he passed away just 24 months into his "golden years." Our assessment is that he hadn't prepared himself for a whole new lifestyle. It happens to a lot of people after they retire. They haven't been thinking strategically. Consequently the effects on them and their families are devastating. We have talked to people who say their spouses are driving them crazy since the spouse retired because they are suddenly together all of the time. It is an unfortunate reality when dynamics of a relationship change and the people involved are not prepared for the change.

But whether it is retirement or something else, you have to think about your mind, body, and spirit to sustain the energy you  will need for success in the long run. These needs are not born out of greed. Rather, they are born out of the desire to be in the best condition possible in order to withstand the changes and demands of work and customers, find some joy in work, and make a contribution in life. You need the strength to do battle with the future, and to do this you must develop and sharpen your skills. You need to enhance your creativity and flexibility. You need to meditate and reflect. It is essential that you nourish your values and beliefs, and that you live in balance with your principles. Your self-esteem and your motivational needs are important to sustained success. Building your inner awareness will help you diagnose your personal requirements as you move forward. You need to cultivate healthy life practices and promote your physical, emotional, and mental wellness. Managing your economic situation will help you avoid being unduly encumbered by the future in a way that limits your options or creates frustration and conflict. Most importantly, you need to develop a picture of the future, see how you fit in it, and decide what you should be doing today to be successful in the future and a value-added contributor.

> "Burnout happens, not because we're trying to solve problems, but because we're trying to solve the same problem over and over."
>
> *Susan Scott*

7. SPONSORS/STAKEHOLDERS

Sometimes overlooked are the parties and constituencies who have entrusted us with their money, security, and hopes for the future: the SPONSORS/STAKEHOLDERS. We believe that sound strategic thinking has to take our stewardship of this dashboard area into account. At the end of the day, we have to ask ourselves if we are looking out for the investor, student, donor, or citizen who is risking something to support our work. Whether it is business, government, research, or education, we owe someone something in return for their investment or contribution. If it is a sound profit, then we have to look for ways to provide not only immediate but long-term sustained growth and profitability. If our stakeholders are constituents or citizens, we must ask ourselves similar tough questions such as "Are they getting their money's worth from hard earned tax dollars?" We should look at our work from an entrepreneurial perspective. Unfortunately, too many investors want a fast return, a quick fix, and instant relief. Life and work don't usually work that way, but strategic thinkers are busy getting set for the future, discovering what these interest groups need and want. They care about serving those who make their jobs possible.

> "Far too many executives have become more concerned with the 'four P's' — pay, perks, power, prestige — rather than making profits for shareholders."
>
> *T. Boone Pickens*
> *Chairman of Mesa*
> *Petroleum*

These seven dashboard areas represent the hunting ground for your strategic targets. Reviewing them will help you get a strategic target in your sights. Select an area that feels right and is interesting or exciting for you to pursue. This doesn't require any kind of planning at this point. It only requires a clear picture of the target that you select from the dashboard area.

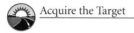

A C.L.E.A.R. Target.

We are often asked what a clear target looks like. It is pretty simple. In fact, nothing about strategic thinking is all that complex. A good target that is well defined has a certain profile. We like to describe it as criteria for a C.L.E.A.R. target.

> "A good target that is well defined has a certain profile."

C = **Controllable.** Something you have control over. It doesn't mean that you control every aspect, but it does mean that you are relatively free to choose and act on the strategic target that has surfaced. The target should be within your scope of responsibility and authority.

L = **Linked.** Smart strategic thinkers are aware of the organization as a whole. They don't act unilaterally; rather, they search out information and choose a strategic course of action that aligns with what the organization is trying to accomplish strategically.

Controllable
Linked
Energizing
Actionable
Result-Oriented

This means that if the business is moving into "Y" technology, you don't invest heavily or train extensively in "X" technology. However, you aren't precluded from staying abreast of "X" technology or being prepared if the organization decides to shift to "X" technology. It just means you use good judgment and consider the environment you are operating in.

E = **Energizing.** A good strategic target has to be something you want to go after. You stand a better chance over the long haul if the target initiative is exciting, fun, and rewarding. If your target is more important than exciting, then the importance aspect will have to drive you in your pursuit of the target. If a target isn't inherently motivating for you, it is less likely that you will be devoted to it.

A = **Actionable.** Once you have gathered the data, analyzed it, and thought the process through, you will be able to create a plan of action for your target area that can be reasonably implemented. It means you have the resources and energy to invest in the campaign. In short, attaining the target is doable with your actions and behaviors.

R = Result-Oriented. Your strategic target should make a difference in your performance results. You will have clearly identified the results of your target if you can accurately respond to questions like these: What does this target do that drives your personal value to your customer and product? What will this new position achieve? What are the downside risks and negative consequences associated with this initiative? Is it worth risking the negative consequences? Does this target contribute to your vision and mission, to what you want the future to look like? Will this initiative put you on an innovated track? Given what you have to trade off or invest, is it a good deal?

As you get your bearings and begin to articulate the target, see if it fits the C.L.E.A.R. standard. If it doesn't, keep working and refining the description of the target until it is crystal clear. Then formulate a clear statement that identifies what you are seeking to improve and explains the future you want to create.

The historical battleground of Gettysburg is full of examples of people who demonstrated the skills of applied strategic thinking. Gettysburg is close to our hearts because we have examined  the applied strategies that took place at this historic site. In fact, we often teach applied strategic thinking workshops at this location. For example, Brigadier General John Buford is the perfect example of a leader who effectively "acquired a target."

One of the first to arrive on the outskirts of Gettysburg with his 2,750 men, John Buford started "reconnoitering" his resources. On June 30, he dispatched an experienced cavalry officer to explore the area. From this exploration, his own observations, and reports from farmers and scouts, Buford learned that several Confederate divisions, some 6,000-8,000 strong, were also converging on Gettysburg. Based on this analysis of the geography, he determined that his strategic target was finding the best terrain for his troops to defend, and he called it the "high ground" south of town. As a result of concentrating on the high ground, he was able to buy valuable time while large numbers of Federal reinforcements could arrive from Washington, D.C. Buford was clear about his target. This example can be applied to your own situation and the battles you will face in the future. Explore your entire field of opportunity so you can effectively acquire your own "high ground."

> "You'll have to fight like the devil to hold your own. . ."
> *General John Buford*
> *Union Brigadier*
> *General*

CONCLUSION

The dashboard is where you search for targets and I.D.A.s of interest. The dashboard areas combine in a unique way to produce optimum levels of success over time. Strategic thinkers always have one eye on the dashboard because they know these seven areas are the ingredients of success and that targets come and go. If you trust the dashboard, it will help you locate a worthy target to exploit.

This step in the process doesn't have to be complicated. The first phase is designed to locate an area or field of focus (what is important to you and the success of your function). In the second phase, reflect on your mission (mission analysis); what do you want to be, do, or have? In the third phase, you can take a shot at defining the initial target, opportunity, or concern (given where you are now, where do you want to be in the future that will yield benefits?). So describe it, name it, identify it, crystallize it, and make it concrete.

Once you have your point on the horizon locked in, you can do a quick check to make sure it is truly strategic. Here is the litmus test, or questions for your target:

1. Will your I.D.A. produce valuable results in the long run?

2. Will this I.D.A. cause you to do new things or do existing things in a new way?

3. Did you discover this I.D.A. or did someone else instruct you to do it?

> "If you can find a path with no obstacles, it probably doesn't lead anywhere."
>
> *Frank A. Clark*
> *American Author*

4. Will this I.D.A. stir up some controversy or resistance?

5. Are there some risks and uncertainties associated with this I.D.A.?

6. Are you willing to support the I.D.A. through trials and challenges?

7. Will this I.D.A. help liberate me from the tyranny of the operating beast or gorilla?

Wayne Gretzky, the famous hockey player, once said, "The key to success is not skating to where the puck is, but to where it is going to be." So, you have to think ahead and anticipate where the future target will be. What we are talking about in this chapter is your navigation system. Use your navigation system to look at targets from every angle. Try to find the "good" prey, not the "easy" prey. Picking the right target is so important because it will be your source of inspiration as you push forward.

CHAPTER SIX

Gather Intelligence

6

Gather Intelligence

"Our business in life is not to get ahead of others, but to get ahead of ourselves; to break our own records; to outstrip our yesterdays by our todays; to bear our trials more beautifully than we ever dreamed we could; to give as we never have given; to do our work with more force and a finer finish than ever. This is the true idea: to get ahead of ourselves."

Carl Holmes

Let's assume that you have been successful in locating a significant strategic target, and you have a clear picture of what you would like to have happen at some point down the road. You can now turn your attention to the next element in the strategic thought process: gathering intelligence. This is also an important element of the process, because so many of the other steps rely on good intelligence. You don't want to pursue a target where you have little knowledge about how the game is played.

Intelligence is all about putting your finger on the pulse of your environment and turning information into knowledge, knowledge into decisions, and decisions into action. Gathering intelligence enables you to see the patterns and forces taking shape that will influence the future.

We have said before that strategy is a lot like warfare. It is about winning the battle against the future and against substitutes or alternatives to our products or services. If you were a company, it would be about winning the "market share," growing the

business, and outpacing the competition. In practical and personal strategic terms, it is a little different. It is about branding yourself or your team and succeeding in building a better, more productive future. In order to do that, you need to conduct a reconnaissance mission around the strategic target that is now in your sights. In fact, reconnaissance or intelligence gathering takes place on at least two levels. The first, Level One, is specific intelligence about the C.L.E.A.R. target you have created. You should also keep in mind that successful stra-

> "It is wiser to find out than to suppose."
> *Mark Twain*
> *American Humorist*
> *and Writer*

tegic thinkers are also gathering data about the forces in the environment and about their own resources required to implement and sustain a plan. This is Level Two intelligence. Level Two intelligence is broader in nature, and we will focus on it first.

Level Two Intelligence

Level Two is "continuous reconnaissance," constantly having your mental radar sweep across the broad spectrum of your organization, the industry, and in fact, the world. It means taking a healthy interest in news, professional developments, and breakthroughs that are happening around the world. Specifically, you need to be alert to events and "shocks," which can positively or negatively disrupt your world and put a new order to things in your field of work. This could be something as basic as sensing that your business is about to reorganize, that new technology is about to be rolled out, or that a government regulation is about to change.

We find current events interesting and engaging, and when we are working on a project, we often have the news channel on as a backdrop, just as some people use music as a working background. You may find it bizarre, but it is our way of staying connected to the world around us. Some of you may find Level Two intelligence gathering easy to do, and to others it may seem like a chore. But there are, in fact, a lot of sources for Level Two reconnaissance. In Peter Schwartz's book, *The Art of the Long View,* he describes many potential Level Two data sources, including magazines such as *Discover, The Economist, Foreign Affairs, Harper's Magazine, British New Scientist, Scientific American,* and *Technology Review,* to name a few. We also find the *Strategic Journal* useful. You will need to find the sources of information that pertain to you and the innovations that may impact your own situation.

However, in gathering information, you need to avoid the trap of paying total attention to a "broadband" of intelligence from sources that you deem as personally or politically correct, the ones that agree with your personal philosophy. It is essential to embrace diversity and to hear other perspectives and multiple points of view in order to have a full picture and to anticipate alternative scenarios. You never know what will prove to be a valuable source of information for you or to spur your thoughts in a productive direction. Good strategic thinkers learn to take their cues from a continuous stream of reconnaissance. At times you may feel like you need a "personal intelligence committee." But in fact, your good sources will actually serve as your personal committee.

> "The test of a first-rate intelligence is the ability to hold two opposed ideas in the mind at the same time, and still retain the ability to function."
>
> *The Great Gatsby*
> *Francis Scott*
> *Fitzgerald*
> *American Author*

Level One Intelligence

With Level Two as a backdrop, let's take a look at Level One reconnaissance. Keep in mind that both levels will help you spot trends and see relationships between and implications of events. This information is your harbinger of the future, and it will help you to make some reasonable assumptions and longer term forecasts about the future. Gathering intelligence is not looking into a mystical crystal ball; it is a very practical and natural thing to do. Those who concentrate on gathering priceless intelligence about their target increase the possibility of spotting "golden opportunities" that provide a tail wind as they journey to the target. They see windows of opportunity open and close. They can see storms blowing in on the horizon and can batten down the hatches before the boat fills with water. Intelligence is simply a way of taking the pulse of your situation. It is nothing more than a process of acquiring and analyzing relevant data.

"There is one thing even more vital to science than intelligent methods; and that is the sincere desire to find out the truth, whatever it may be."

Charles Pierce
American Journalist

The unique aspect of Level One intelligence gathering is that it needs to be going on all the time, because again, it feeds all of the other elements of the strategic thinking process. It gives you specific insight about the target, it provides the feedstock for building future scenarios, it supplies the raw material to spot opportunities and threats, and it helps you implement your plan of action as you journey out to achieve the target objective.

Level One intelligence allows you to profile the target's key dimensions, characteristics, and features. Gathering and inventorying data requires hard work and can be frustrating because you will miss some things. Some information about opportunities or hazards will fly right in under your radar screen. When it comes to "divining" the future, there will always be unknowns and uncertainties. Good intelligence doesn't mean you will bat a thousand. You just want to get a little better all the time, catch more opportunities, and duck more "flying bricks." When you periodically look up, look out, and interpret the environment around you, patterns will begin to emerge. One thing for sure is that some patterns are

> "One of the functions of intelligence is to take account of the dangers that come from trusting solely to the intelligence."
>
> *Lewis Mumford*
> *American Writer*

more difficult to see than others. It is easier, for example, to predict a hurricane than it is to predict an earthquake. However, over time you will learn what causes certain things to happen. You will become more proficient at spotting true causal patterns, rather than simple or unusual coincidences. Understanding these causal factors will help you reach your destination. So before you move forward on your strategic expedition, awaken your senses about the future that is rapidly flying at you.

Using the Intelligence You Gather

So how do you get good at reading the road signs and converting information and clues about the future into knowledge that can work for you? First, assess the information your have about your target. Literally take a moment and write down what you currently know and understand about the strategic target. Don't evalu- 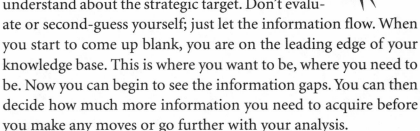 ate or second-guess yourself; just let the information flow. When you start to come up blank, you are on the leading edge of your knowledge base. This is where you want to be, where you need to be. Now you can begin to see the information gaps. You can then decide how much more information you need to acquire before you make any moves or go further with your analysis.

As you explore what you know, you may actually discover  you do have enough experience and information to move to the next phase of strategic thinking. On the other hand, you may discover that you have a lot of work to do and that a lot of learning has to occur. If the latter is the case, you will need to find a subject matter expert, or you will need an ally who can guide, advise, and inform you. At this

stage, you don't want experts taking over your strategic campaign. You just want them to weigh in with their information and listen to opposing points of view. Whether it is your information or someone else's, lay it on the table and identify the assumptions. After talking to the subject matter experts about your target, seek out other information, options, and insights from your customers, team members, and other allies. Check out the literature and do some research. Remember that this is the learning stage, so don't be afraid to own up and admit to your information gaps. One

> "I'm not the smartest fellow in the world, but I can sure pick smart colleagues."
> *Franklin D. Roosevelt*
> *32nd President of*
> *the United States*

of our mentors, Cal Taylor, would say, "You have to be willing to be a novice." We believe that means that you have to let go of some ego, be a bit humble, and open your mind to new data.

This phase of intelligence gathering requires an investment on your part. It may require some resources, or it may simply cost your ego a little bit to ask for help, to probe others, and to pick the brains of people in the know. Doing some research will do a lot of good, but don't trust everything you hear; experts can be wrong at times. Karl von Clausewitz, a writer on military strategy, has a rather negative view of intelligence. He says, "A great part of the information obtained in war is contradictory, a greater part of it is false, and by far the greatest part is of doubtful character." These are awfully strong words, maybe too cynical. It seems that it would be better to have more rather than less data; then you can decide what to pay attention to. You can bounce new ideas off your own experience and continue the thought process with a wealth of information.

If you have a lot of information, it might be beneficial to organize it into a more user-friendly format. You can categorize the data into "buckets" or into a two dimensional diagram. Mind mapping or fishbone diagrams are other good ways of making sense of the intelligence. The traditional fishbone uses historical pat-

> "Information is a source of learning. But unless it is organized, processed, and available to the right people in a format for decision making, it is a burden not a benefit."
>
> *William Pollard*

terns to create a visual picture of the past. A strategic fishbone is future oriented: the head of the fish is your target, and the bones represent key dimensions or aspects of the target. Post the information or intelligence you have around the bones or categories, thus revealing the bare bones. This is where you need to add more data in order to proceed through the strategic thought process. This is your opportunity to see the gaps, identify the irregularities, and even be surprised by the signals you are picking up. Avoid drawing any conclusions at this stage; just find and fill information gaps while identifying what you do and don't know about this target.

Evaluate Data

Now you can begin the final part of intelligence gathering – perhaps the most important part. This is when you focus on translating information and distilling the signals you are picking up. You ask yourself, "What is the data telling me?" or "What do the signals suggest or indicate?" Maybe you will find a repeating pattern or cycle that is meaningful. With that information, you can dig deeper to find out if the patterns are predictable, stable, and lasting over time. You may have to do some "if…then" thinking to see if a pattern exists. Historical data or lagging indicators may provide a helpful cause-and-effect forecasting tool. Some people are able to

understand the past and dominate the future. But in many cases, you may need leading indicators that correlate with and foretell the future. Unfortunately, some people base their predictions on past data that produced "today," not on data that will produce "tomorrow." So take a balanced approach as you consider

information about the future. There may be a variety of ways to diagnose the future and determine a prescription for action or a prescription to wait out a storm and keep your "action plan" in port. Part of the task will be to discover the significance and implications of the data. You will need to sort out what intelligence is central to your target and the journey ahead and what is peripheral.

At a practical level, creating a barometer for the future is not "rocket science." It doesn't take a Ph.D. statistician, for example, to observe that most teenage driving accidents occur right after school in the chaotic parking lot when the law of the jungle is the only traffic regulation in force. These accidents occur every day at our local high schools when a thousand inexperienced drivers descend on the parking lot. If we were in charge of safety and security at a school, we would recommend avoiding the parking lot at 3:30 p.m. during school days.

> "Knowing a great deal is not the same as being smart; intelligence is not information alone but also judgment, the manner in which information is collected and used."
>
> *Dr. Carl Sagan*
> *American Scientist*
> *and Writer*

Often it takes a simple observation or a search for relationships and commonalities in the data to draw inferences. Again, you don't have to be clairvoyant, seek after mystical omens, or read cards. You just have to ask yourself some basic questions:

- Does anybody care if 'X' happens and 'Y' is the result?
- Should I pay attention to the data and be prepared for future 'X' events?
- Is an 'X' event worth taking action on?
- Do I need to be proactive and try to turn 'X' events into 'Z' events instead?
- Do I try to simply avoid 'X' at all costs?

Some people say everything you do comes down to your ability to understand, predict, and control the future. In some cases, you may never know why "X" happens, so you work with it as a given; but you don't give up completely on influencing the future.

You can always check the data against other known patterns and relationships by using existing models and templates to help you anticipate the future. At a minimum, you can begin to sort the information, identify the emerging picture, and see the forces that will be working on your target. Having good intelligence won't give you 20-20 future vision. There will definitely be times when you will have to "drive through smoke," as NASCAR drivers refer to it when you can't see what is up ahead and you have to muster the courage to go on anyway.

CONCLUSION

Get ahead of the curve by getting on the information express now. Keep abreast of social, economic, political, and global trends that will help you anticipate what you can expect to see as future workplace evolutions occur. Study meaningful news, read the journals, and keep your finger on the pulse of society. As you do, many changes, challenges, and opportunities won't come as surprises to you. Eventually, you will become more pro-active and in control of your situation without so much stress. As you get a handle on the intelligence and the variables at play, you can distill the patterns, look for cycles and connections, and identify potential cause-and-effect relationships. You will then be better equipped to delve further into the applied strategic thinking process.

Let's face it, nearly everything around you, including yourself, has a limited life expectancy. Thoughtful intelligence can give you the "lead time" so you can act early, before things become outmoded. As you think about your information, you will be able to make preparations, identify important obstacles that may trip you up, and search for interesting opportunities that will pave

your way to greater success. But no matter how good you are at prognosticating, the future will sometimes develop in unforeseeable ways. You may be able to see the precursors of disaster and maybe you won't. It's what makes the future exciting and challenging to manage.

CHAPTER SEVEN

Analyze Forces

7

Analyze Forces

Identify External Forces

Each of you lives and works in a complex and highly unique environment. Your surroundings provide a web of advantages, favorable circumstances, and tailwinds, as well as storms to navigate through and headwinds to defy. Strategic people learn to leverage these external advantages and neutralize the environmental threats in order to survive and thrive.

> "Strategic people learn to leverage these external advantages and neutralize the environmental threats in order to survive and thrive."

In the external environment, you have little direct control over many of the complex factors and forces swirling around you. However, you can exercise indirect control over the forces that are pushing and pulling on you, influencing your decisions, targets, and plans.

Just like the masters teach in the martial arts, you have to learn how to manage the forces coming at you and effectively channel them to the best of your ability. The thing you don't want to do is confront these forces head on, resulting in a catastrophic collision. Successful strategic work is developing the capacity to understand, nurture, cultivate, and influence these forces rather than compelling, coercing, and forcing the environment to serve your needs and circumstances.

The key is to learn how to anticipate, understand, and adapt to the positive and negative energy that you will inevitably have to contend with. There are really two choices; you can fight (strive) against the forces, or you can manage and harness these forces to the degree that is possible and practical.

External Threats (Hazards)

Many great books have been written to help people understand and cope with failure. We agree that turning setbacks into successes will help you be more productive and prosperous. Although overcoming failure is a vital leadership skill, this chapter focuses more on how to avoid failure and making mistakes in the first place. Some people may have a philosophical difference with us regarding this part of the chapter. Other people are fanatical about the notion that long-term success is largely influenced by your capacity to withstand defeat and that you should focus your energies on opportunities rather than obstacles. Our belief is that if you can accurately recognize obstacles, threats, or mistakes that are on the horizon before it happens, you will save a lot of energy that can be directed into pursuing promising opportunities. Specifically, threats are the risks and adverse conditions in the external environment that will be a barrier to the achievement of your strategic target. So what becomes important is focusing on how to understand, evaluate, and manage threats before they turn into trials.

> "If you can accurately recognize obstacles, threats, or a mistake on the horizon before it happens, you will save a lot of energy that can be directed into pursuing promising opportunities."

Now obviously this won't always be possible. Without question, we will all make missteps, need to pick ourselves up off the road, and find the motivation to continue on. But at this stage of the strategic process, it is the ability to spot a pothole before you hit it that is important. It is also the ability to work through the fear of failure that could potentially stop you in your tracks and cause you to give up without even trying to achieve your strategic target. But ironically, adversity and failure can provide you with the strength to ensure long-term success.

Recognizing Threats (Hazards)

There are a few straightforward principles for recognizing and evaluating threats. The place to start is to review and examine your intelligence data in depth. We can't stress enough the importance of having a radar that is continually gathering information about potential hazards and potential risks. To be sure, your radar may send you  false or misleading signals; it may be recognizing everything or nothing as a threat. After all, we are talking about the future, which is filled with many unknowns. You need the ability to discern what

is a legitimate concern for your endeavor and what is a mirage. Good strategists have an uncanny ability to isolate realistic threats and do something about them. A lot can go wrong on your strategic journey when decisions are made on the basis of a poor understanding of your environment. Using your best reconnaissance, make a list of all of the threats that

"Good strategists have an uncanny ability to isolate realistic threats and do something about them."

you can see from your data. You may create a warehouse full of potential trouble areas. That is okay. Don't worry if some of the threats appear unlikely or irratio-

nal at this point. Let your mind go, dump them all out, and leave no stone unturned. You may find it cathartic to let your mind empty out all possible concerns.

Evaluating Threats (Hazards)

The next step requires you to rationally evaluate your list of possible threats. You will want to search for relevant and likely threats. Some threats or forces working against you simply need to be observed and monitored. Some of life's storms and disrup-

tions, for example, will simply move around you and have little impact. Other risks and challenges you simply tolerate, preparing for a battering that can't be avoided. The cost of trying to alter these external forces is not worth it: the cost is too high or the obstacles too strong to try to change or dance around them. Other risks and hazards can be prevented with well-placed actions and investments. Certain threats can be mitigated or minimized in those cases where misfortune does occur. You can always have a contingency plan or a fallback position that you can resort to for protection and safety. It reminds us of a hurricane. People in the path of a hurricane first have to decide if they are in the direct path of the storm. Then they determine whether they should stay in their homes, board up, and wait it out, or evacuate to higher ground until the storm has passed.

> "Life's ups and downs provide windows of opportunity to determine your values and goals – think of using all obstacles as stepping stones to build the life you want."
>
> *Marsha Sinetar*
> *Author*

So, define and reflect on each threat that you have identified. Ask yourself, "What threats are specific and relevant to my strategic target?" Label the threats and then discard or set aside those threats that are not relevant. Too many people cripple themselves before they even begin a strategic journey by allowing their imaginations to control them through outrageous and irrelevant threats. These threats might apply to some other journey but are not related to the one they are initiating.

Now that you have labeled and sorted the threats, you need to evaluate the seriousness or potential impact of the hazards that remain on your radar screen. Ask yourself if they pose a substantial threat or a minor threat. You can actually rate how devastating or impactful they might be (1 to 10, with 1 being an irritation and 10 being a devastation). Ask others to check your perception and numbers. Somehow you need to validate your interpretation of the threat.

At this point you are ready to assess the probability of occurrence. In other words, is it highly likely, somewhat likely, or unlikely
that a major or minor threat will really happen? You can be less
worried about hazards that have a low probability of occurrence
and devote your energy to preparing for more likely occurrences
that will have a greater impact.

To ensure you are prepared for the threats you might face on
your strategic journey, determine what systems or signals will help
alert you that a threat is developing. You may have seen Doppler
radar technology on weather programs. When green dots or patterns begin to appear on the radar, they are an indicator that a
storm is on the horizon. And so it is with your external threats.

> "You just need to
> know what may be
> on the path ahead
> if you pursue this
> journey."

Again, the objective is to search out specific,
relevant, impactful, and likely threats.
Through this process, you will discover that
some threats should be factored into the planning process and given some attention. But
don't get overly fixated on them. They don't
need to divert your focus from the target at
this stage. You just need to know what may be on the path ahead
if you pursue this journey and then make some preparation be-
forehand. Being smart and ready for what you can see coming
gives you the best chance of success in reaching your target.

External Advantages (Tailwinds)

On the other side of the equation are the positive driving
forces that are working in your behalf. Advantages are the favorable conditions in your external environment worth pursuing or
utilizing. Using the same process as for identifying threats, you
need to scour your intelligence to pinpoint potential or under-
developed advantages. Allow your mind to be creative and explore a variety of areas where there are advantages that may not
be in plain view. Good strategic thinkers are able to identify even
obscure advantages that are tucked away out of sight.

Francis Bacon said, "A wise man will make more opportunities than he finds." This is often true when it comes to identifying strategic advantages. You may be searching for situations that you can convert into advantages instead of already developed advantages that you hopefully stumble across. Advantages may not just appear magically in your mind. You may need to let the advantage seeds that you have planted incubate and develop over a period of time.

> "You may need to let the opportunity seeds that you have planted incubate and develop over a period of time."

Have you ever read Aesop's fable called "The Grasshopper and the Ants?" It goes like this:

One fine day in winter some Ants were busy drying their store of corn, which had gotten rather damp during a long spell of rain. Presently a Grasshopper came up and begged them to spare her a few grains. "For," she said, "I'm simply starving."

The Ants stopped work for a moment, though this was against their principles. "May we ask," said they, "what you were doing with yourself all last summer? Why didn't you collect a store of food for the winter?"

"The fact is," replied the Grasshopper, "I was so busy singing that I hadn't the time."

"If you spent the summer singing," replied the Ants, "you can't do better than to spend the winter dancing." And they chuckled and went on with their work.

The moral of the story is "Never lose a good opportunity to take advantage of something." And so it is in your strategic endeavors: you have to be astute and focused enough to identify and take advantage of situations before you are derailed from your strategic path. The grasshopper had fortuitous weather during the summer and simply didn't take advantage of it.

Once again, screen and evaluate the likelihood of a beneficial advantage or good fortune occurring. Some situations simply need to be observed and monitored. These advantages are good to have because no direct investment or energy is required. You can just relax and let the advantages occur naturally. On the other hand, advantages will occur where you will want to shape, cultivate, and exploit the situation to your benefit (which is something the grasshopper failed to do). You can ask yourself if the payoff for this advantage is worth the investment needed to pursue it. Once you have built your list of potential advantages, you can begin to zero in and formulate some ideas about how you can leverage attractive and likely advantages. As is the case with external threats, ensure that you have identified the signs or evidence that signify an advantage is opening up. Ask yourself, "How will I recognize the advantage?" You will even want to think about what might cause you to miss an advantage that comes up. Later in the strategic thinking process, you will build your advantage assessment and indicators into your plan of action (chart a course) for reaching your target.

> "Most successful men have not achieved their distinction by some new talent or opportunity presented to them. They have developed the opportunity at hand."
>
> *Bruce Marton*
> *American Author*

One person we studied, Jill, has a knack for thinking strategically. Jill is the facilities and security director for a large company that develops and produces high-tech devices for the electronics industry. Jill has an unenviable job because it seems like none of her internal customers are ever happy with their facilities. Unless Jill is continually ahead of the curve, things can turn ugly in a hurry when high-priced engineers and scientists start running out of lab space and computer lines. Jill has had to be especially good at collecting and interpreting intelligence that alerts her to advantages and threats occuring in her environment.

For several months, Jill was listening to the signals coming through her system of gathering intelligence. Generally speaking, all the indicators at a global level were signaling that the industry was heating up. Furthermore, Jill's company was beginning to accelerate and experience more success than the average company in the sophisticated electronics and communication industry. So the global political and economic indicators, combined with industry indicators, were suggesting that if the facilities groups didn't think creatively and well ahead of the curve, the company would move its expansion to some other location with more abundant physical space.

No one contacted Jill to let her know of possible upcoming changes or advantages opening up for her location. But Jill was astute, thinking strategically, and she continued to monitor the data from Human Resources. As the facility started hiring one engineer per week, she was ready with a solution. When the Operations VP asked how the facilities group would handle all of the growth, Jill was prepared with options. Because she had been thinking ahead of the curve, she had streamlined her own organization in preparation for change. In addition, Jill had already begun to locate and make job offers to mechanical engineers and architects who could plan for major expansion efforts. Because Jill saw an advantage to pursue, her team had begun a ritual of looking at handling the growth in creative ways that enhanced synergy rather than detracted from it. Jill and her team recognized the need for clear communication lines between lab workers and engineers. They developed the innovative idea of leasing 250,000 square feet of space and contracting with two other locations with an all-weather elevated skywalk that would facilitate easy access between two

> "Most people don't recognize opportunity when it comes, because it's usually dressed in overalls and looks a lot like work."
>
> *Thomas Alva Edison*
> *American Inventor*

major research groups. While most people were complaining about the heating and cooling systems or the lack of lighting, some of Jill's team were paying attention to the signals, had seen the advantages and threats, and were ready to act. They had even prepared a backup plan in case the global market collapsed by negotiating the lease of the 250,000-square-foot facility for only two years, rather than for the customary five years. This positioned Jill to adjust easily in case the business had to downsize.

There are many similar examples, but suffice it to say, Jill was on top of her game, routinely thinking ahead of the curve despite the day-to-day firefighting of keeping the temperature regulated, the lights on, and the facilities secure. Jill understood that being a  good day-to-day operator wouldn't ensure her success or that of her team. No question, her success required some innovative thinking and some risks. In fact, some people thought she was crazy when she asked the legal department to help negotiate a lease on space several months before the demand hit. Yes, Jill could have been wrong, but when you think about the cost of doing nothing, acting strategically was the best decision.

Unfortunately, some people fly right into the eye of a big storm, totally unaware of what they are doing. Others fly right past a great advantage and don't even know it. Strategic people choose which storms are worth taking on and which situations contain high-value advantages to pursue. Like most of the steps in the strategic thinking process, it takes good personal intelligence to see the forces in action. You have to set up listening posts and barometers to monitor the climate and see the patterns and changes that surround you. You also have to muster the courage to pursue an opportunity when the window is open and you get the "advantage alert." Sometimes the fear of failure may keep you from pursuing a really good advantage. The problem is that both

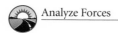

threats and advantages have associated risks. You have to learn to assess the risks and benefits. If the tradeoffs look acceptable, you press on knowing that one can never be completely prepared for every external force.

As we have indicated before, you won't be able to see and diagnose every force working for or against you. Strategic thinking is often imperfect. But you can and will recognize more of these external forces, be able to think clearly about what they can do to you or for you, and become better at managing them if you practice these key ideas and skills.

Internal Forces

Now, let's move to the "internal" forces. People who live and operate strategically have a realistic understanding of their weaknesses and limitations (headwinds) as well as their inherent strengths and capabilities (tailwinds). They are good at applying and leveraging their strengths and managing or neutralizing their weaknesses. Your natural strengths and limitations create boundaries and help you decide which targets can be pursued and which may be out of reach at a given moment in time.

 This means thinking and operating within a logical and reasonable framework of reality. We don't fully subscribe to the popular notion that, "If you can conceive it, you can achieve it." While it is heartwarming to believe that achieving any strategic target is possible, it isn't always realistic. Operating on the notion that anyone can do anything, that the sky's the limit, is sometimes frustrating and dangerous.

This certainly doesn't mean that you shouldn't push the limits or stretch to achieve

"Exploration of the full range of our own potentialities is not something that we can safely leave to the chances of life. It is something to be pursued avidly to the end of our days."

John W. Gardner
American Writer and
Secretary of Health,
Education, and
Welfare.

goals. Each of you has different capabilities and your own special package of material possessions, personal talents, and gifts. Smart people look at their targets and realistically compare them to their package of personal resources. Strategic people don't waste a lot of time on campaigns that don't reflect their "strength profile."

We had an opportunity to work with a sales and marketing manager in China a couple of years ago. This manager saw an economic expansion war coming his way. He wanted to be prepared and in position to take advantage of the opportunities for the company. He read the signs and made his forecast. He established five strategic targets:

1. Improve internal organization effectiveness.

2. Expand geographically into new regions and areas in China.

3. Improve the territory management skills of the sales team members.

4. Enhance cooperation, coordination, and teamwork between the product marketing and the field sales force.

5. Improve customer satisfaction scores.

Clearly, he could see a number of ambitious targets, and they all looked very attractive. However, Chen was smart; he knew he was a very talented and prolific trainer with a lot of experience. He also had a number of training programs available from the home office that would cost him very little. He knew that budgets would be tight in the foreseeable future because of some product recalls on a global level. In short, Chen began to conduct a simple yet effective resource analysis.

Chen foresaw that his best target was to concentrate efforts and resources on improving the territory management skills of his field force. This target also fit his strength profile. Next on his list was to turn the organization into a smoothly running, "well oiled" machine by improving coordination between sales and marketing. This move was, again, something that wouldn't require more people or a lot of money.

Chen decided to put geographic expansion and customer satisfaction issues on hold for the moment. These would be worthy and ambitious strategic targets to pursue once the business was running on all cylinders. Chen chose wisely, matching the targets within his strength and limitation profile.

Thinking and being strategic means that you take the right risks and pursue a path that can lead to success, rather than frustration and disappointment. It all comes back to balance: a balance between the power of positive thinking and reality, and a balance between hard work, determination, and natural abilities. There is no need to exclusively subscribe to either school of thought. The key is to blend a little positive thinking with your strengths and advantages.

For many people, including us, scuba diving is a favorite pastime. To ensure safety, scuba diving requires some skill and training. To dive effectively you need to be skillful at using and balancing opposing forces. The two forces are weight versus buoyancy (sinking vs. floating). Even with all the hardware you need to scuba dive, some additional weight is needed to help

> "The greatest achievement of the human spirit is to live up to one's opportunities and make the most of one's resources."
> *Marquis de Vauvenargues*
> *18th Century French Moralist and Essayist*

you sink. Many scuba divers like to begin their dive by descending from the surface as soon as they can after entering the water because of the "chop" on the surface, so weight is a very important resource. However, once at the bottom, divers will want to stop sinking and start hovering just above the coral bottom. Therefore, by applying the forces of flotation, adding a little air into their buoyancy system, divers can maintain their depth objective. When returning to the surface, it is vital to add a lot of air into the buoyancy system to stabilize oneself and avoid any chance of sinking oneself. The extra metal weights become the enemy at this point. So, as with

any strategic thinking endeavor; at one moment a strength may seem like a weakness, and in another moment, a weakness may seem like a strength. When you start a dive, you need the weight; when you end a dive, you need the flotation.

When you analyze your internal resources, you are determining how well your strategic target or task matches your strength profile. You identify and sort out the strengths and assets that will aid your journey. This may be one of the most important phases of the entire strategic thinking process. You certainly don't want to disservice yourself or those around you by launching a foray into unknown or risky territory without an understanding of the assets that you can bring to bear on the situation. Likewise, you must have a grasp of the liabilities and disadvantages in your resource package. This side of the equation will be addressed later in the chapter.

> "Identify and sort out the strengths and assets that will aid your journey."

Strengths

In order to determine the appropriate fit between your target and your resource package, you need to unearth and inventory what you can bring to the table. Strengths are more than attitudes and hard work. Strength is not necessarily the opposite of a weakness—they are two separate things. We do believe that each person's situation is very unique and your exclusive package of strengths gives you the capacity to achieve your own strategic mission, plans, and targets. Strengths generally fall into two categories:

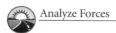

1. "Soft" Resources	2. "Hard" Resources
Skills (know-how)	Time
Knowledge	Money or Funding
Experience	Equipment
Relationship Networks	Facilities
Talents	Tools
Gifts	Alliances
Education	Supplies
Wisdom	Materials
Motivation/Desire	Space
Ideas	Technology
PersonalityTemperament	Contacts
Energy	
Confidence	

Managing Your Strengths

The "hardware" or tangible possessions and strengths are usually easier to see and account for because of their physical nature. We suggest that you simply make a list (it helps to actually write it out so you can inspect it visually). Ask yourself, "What are the tangible resources that can help me reach my target?" Then review the list carefully and put a plus (+) by those items that you control and that will play a positive role in reaching the target. Put a zero (0) by those items that will be helpful, and put a minus (-) by those items that are irrelevant to your specific target.

Next, you need to identify your "soft" strengths or resources. As you think about your target, make a list of the intangible qualities you can contribute to the effort. Again, visualize your strengths in your mind, write them down, and then talk to others about them. Don't compare yourself to others or self-censor your capabilities. Your strengths are relative; they are uniquely yours. Simply think about all the things you are capable of and better at in comparison to things that you are not as skillful at. Understanding what you are capable of should provide clarity and remove uncertainty or chaos before you embark on your journey. Writing down your strengths reminds you of what you have to offer. Having your strengths, advantages, and capabilities clearly in mind contributes greatly to your self-confidence. Such a list also provides you with an opportunity to recognize, celebrate, develop, and extend these strengths.

Again, the whole point here is that it doesn't make a lot of sense to go into a strategic battle without the right tools, mind set, and experience. You need enough forethought to know which battles (targets) you are suited for and which you are not. You want to avoid wasting energy and resources on a fight that you cannot win. Knowing your individual strengths will help you fight in those arenas where you are capable of fighting effectively. There is an old cartoon caption that reads, "Don't try to teach a pig to swim; it wastes your time and it annoys the pig." We are not suggesting that you are a pig; we just believe that it is

> "If you have ability in a certain area, why not capitalize on it and improve it and use it?"
>
> *Wilt Chamberlain*
> *NBA Basketball Star*

smarter to work within your zone of strengths when going after strategic targets. It is as important to know which targets to pursue as it is to know which to let go of. Both decisions require courage and forethought based on your assessment of internal resources.

Having examined and connected with your resources, you are now arriving at a tentative decision point. You can begin to evaluate and make some decisions about whether or not you should proceed with the journey based on whether you feel your strengths will provide you with a winning edge. With enough strength, you may even be able to overwhelm or offset your weaknesses in pursuing this particular target.

The key to getting the most from your strengths is to develop and practice them often. Once unearthed and recognized, genuine strengths are something you must regularly invest in and maintain. Strengths need to be exercised. You can't take them for granted. All too often, you focus on fixing your weaknesses. While this is important to do, you can end up creating your biggest weakness by letting your strengths atrophy. In fact, developing a strength could be a strategic target in and of itself.

Weaknesses

Now, what about weaknesses? Once again, the key is to recognize, own up to, and isolate the weaknesses. Simply put, you have to know what you are not good at, and <u>avoid</u> exposing yourself to situations that involve these particular vulnerabilities; otherwise, you have a recipe for failure. We are not suggesting that you avoid risks, experimentation, or stretching outside your competence zone. But when you take aim at a truly strategic target, you need to be on your own field of battle—home court advantage, so to speak. You need to know your limitations and understand how to manage, neutralize, or make limitations irrelevant.

> "Once we know our weaknesses they cease to do us any harm."
>
> *Anonymous*

As with your strengths, you begin by creating an inventory of your tangible liabilities (material), as well as weaknesses in soft qualities (skills and experience gaps). In an effort to be accurate, ask yourself, "Which gaps or limitations will fundamentally expose me to intolerable risks before I embark on the journey?" "Which weaknesses are mildly critical, and which are insignificant?" Concentrate on the "heavy hitters." As you do, analyze ways to manage or neutralize those weaknesses. In actuality you are doing a little pre-planning at this point. In other words, before you actually chart a course, you will want to know if there is a way around the critical weaknesses, but avoid trying to turn a weakness into a strength. If you want to move forward and you have a show-stopping weakness, you will need a plan to manage this serious limitation.

Keep in mind that weaknesses are not something to deny or be embarrassed about. Everyone has weaknesses, and you should not ignore them (focus on the 80/20 rule: 20% of our weakness will account for 80% of your vulnerability). Limitations should not necessarily stop the journey, and you shouldn't always wait until your weakness goes away. The point is that you will always have some weaknesses to pack along. You will always be a little short on intellect, funding, or prior experience. So the critical question is, "Can you manage the weaknesses, and will your strengths win the day as you take on a challenging target?" If you understand your weaknesses, you will know how to approach the target better and how to chart a course that plays to your strengths.

"There is no finer sensation in life than that which comes with victory over one's self. Go forward to a goal of inward achievement, brushing aside all your old internal enemies as you advance."

Vash Young
American Author

This realistic understanding of your drawbacks should not discourage you or create debilitating fear. Understanding your capabilities allows you to make a decision to proceed in spite of your concerns, fears, or hesitation. It is about being smart. You should start your strategic road trip with your eyes wide open and aware, not afraid. You need to understand your options and your odds before you invest by performing a little due diligence on your proposed journey. Be aware of your options before you take on a situation where your weaknesses will be the determining factor in the outcome.

Managing Your Weaknesses

If you have correctly recognized and isolated weaknesses that matter, how can you manage or neutralize these weaknesses? The first rule is: don't move in the direction of a significant weakness. If you know you are not good at something, stop doing it or don't put yourself in a position where you are dependent on a weakness to drive your success. Apply your energy, time, resources, and talents to initiatives that fit your strength profile. Sometimes you want to prove how heroic you can be by laboring onward in the face of big natural weaknesses. Don't do it. Learn to coach yourself out of these unproductive pursuits. Persevering in the face of a major weakness is asking for problems you don't need.

> "Apply your energy, time, resources, and talents to initiatives that fit your strength profile."

Second, have the courage to ask for help if you must press on with your pursuit despite your weaknesses. Look for allies and partners to assist you. If you have a team working for you, consider delegating and enrolling others to counteract your weaknesses. For example, look for opportunities to hire additional temporary talent to get through situations that require more time than you have. Train yourself to let go of the worry and guilt that some people feel when they delegate tasks and activities that are unpleasant or an unnatural fit for them. Too often, you feel you have to be all things to all people — the heroic perfectionist mentality.

Third, look for technology or mechanical solutions that can negate a weakness. So many forms of technology and even software are available that can compensate for weaknesses. Use your creativity as you explore the various options available to you. Sometimes you may stumble upon a solution that proves to be highly effective and truly converts a weakness into a strength. Use your allies and partners to help you identify potential technological or mechanical solutions.

Fourth, explore new and creative ways to bypass your weakness using different paths or approaches. Sometimes you get caught up in logical thinking instead of playing with ideas and thinking about something differently. Roger von Oech, in his book *A Whack on the Side of the Head* said, "Life is like cooking. It all depends on what you add and how you mix it. Sometimes you follow the recipe and at other times you are creative." So use your imagination and be innovative in coming up with alternative approaches to reach your target. This may mean testing boundaries, challenging rules, breaking patterns, or examining the merits of other ideas. One way of doing this is to think about how others might manipulate the situation to bypass a weakness. You may even find that modifying your target a little is a productive and effective approach for detouring around a weakness without totally compromising your desired outcome.

> "Objectives are not fate; they are direction. They are not commands; they are commitments. They do not determine the future; they are means to mobilize the resources and energies of the business for the making of the future."
>
> *Peter Drucker*
> *U.S. Educator and Writer*

Fifth, if your weaknesses are significant and your strengths do not provide enough support for the journey, consider waiting until you are stronger or better equipped. If this is your decision, work towards minimizing the weakness while you wait. Stay active, and don't let your target go by the wayside. Spend some time exploring how you can overcome the situation or develop yourself in this area. In some cases, this may mean getting involved in training, education, practice, or other methods that will help you overcome a weakness or reinforce a strength.

Again, don't let weaknesses completely derail your plan. Concentrate on your strengths while realistically examining your weaknesses. Remember what Peter Drucker, an American business philosopher and author, said: "Strong people typically have strong weaknesses." We believe it is how you handle your strengths and weaknesses that will determine your ultimate level of strategic success.

By knowing what you can and cannot do, you can plan a course of action that will give you the best outcome. The following diagram gives you an idea on how to use your internal forces.

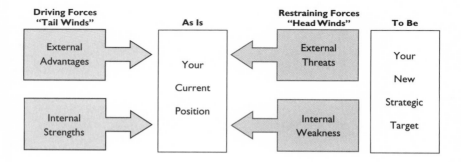

CHAPTER EIGHT

Define Scenarios

8

Define Scenarios

A scenario is a vivid representation of what you think the future environment will be down the road. It is a story line of both the events and outcomes that you can anticipate. It is not just a single forecast, but a range of reasonable or plausible outcomes that could unfold in pursuit of your strategic target. You can't know everything for certain, but you do know something will occur in the future. Now you need to harness all of your intelligence, experience, and know-how, and turn it into a reasonable and knowledgeable prediction about the events that are likely to ensue.

> "Scenarios channel your thought process with regard to opportunities, hazards, and a plan of attack."

Scenarios are important because they channel your thought process with regard to opportunities and hazards into a plan of attack. Alternative descriptions of the likely future will help you recognize and adapt rapidly to changing conditions as the future begins to take shape. If you are better able to see which track the future is on, you can act decisively if disruptions or upheavals occur. Scenarios allow you to prepare now for opportunities and help you make choices based on some reasonable estimate of how events may turn out. You may not recognize it, but opening up your thinking to various stories or plots based on good intelligence and experience will make  future events and results stand out boldly. Creating scenarios is actually a very natural thing to do before you chart a specific course of action.

Scenarios are not dreams, wishes, or visions of hope. They are not abstract, inconsistent, or implausible. Rather they are grounded in reality and based on your research, and they will help you construct plans and make productive decisions. As we said in the last chapter, your future environment is full of forces that will work to your benefit or detriment as you pursue your strategic targets. The ability to look ahead in the face of uncertainty and act on your insights and experience allows you to be prepared for whatever really happens, whether it is positive or negative.

> "Scenarios are not dreams, wishes, or visions of hope."

Peering into the future needs a healthy dose of reality combined with some ability to vividly imagine and visualize where you are headed, what will happen along the route, and what the  final destination will be. Scenarios allow you to assess the uncertainties, complexities, and unpredictability of the future. You need a concrete, realistic view of tomorrow because when you have that in mind you can breathe some life into your plan. Your thinking about ensuing events, players, forces, and results will help you generate scenarios based on data, rather than subjective optimism or pessimism.

The purpose of scenario building at this stage is not to fix or address things you depict in the scenarios. The task at hand is to simply identify, think about, and describe possible outcomes. Later, when you build your action plan, you can formulate ways to enable and facilitate the desired scenarios and avoid the adverse ones. Right now, you just want to view the "reasonable" possibilities. This will enable you to put together a smart course of action to get you to your destination.

Scenario building begins with the intelligence and knowledge you have already gathered. It requires looking at the cause-and-effect relationships and getting a feel for directions the future is taking. Next you need to construct outcomes: a variety of deliverables, destinations, or end points that are likely results of the journey or undertaking. Ask yourself some basic questions at this stage of your thinking, such as, "Where or what will this initiative lead to?" or "What can I expect to have happen if I take this trip or go down that path?" If you can anticipate, project, or foresee the various eventualities and possibilities, you can begin to think of ways to support forward movement as you chart a specific course of action.

The next step in the scenario-building process requires the construction of two scenario possibilities at the most fundamental level. The first scenario to construct is the best "probable" scenario. In other words, what is the data telling you that you can reasonably and optimistically expect? Begin by answering the following types of questions: "Is it possible that

> "Be careful not to deceive yourself with unreasonably optimistic story lines."

this journey could go according to plan?" "If it did, what would a positive outcome look like?" "What will the future be like?" You also need to break down this positive scenario a little further by asking some searching questions that will enable you to identify the causes and drivers (independent variables) that will account for the likely positive scenario. So the question now is very simple: "What would have to happen in order to achieve this probable outcome?" Be careful not to deceive yourself with unreasonably optimistic story lines. You need realistic options to work with, so don't go off the scale. The key word here is probable.

Now you are ready to construct the worst likely scenario. People often refer to this as their "worst case scenario." We caution against that. It may be unproductive to think in worst-case terms if such a scenario has a relatively low likelihood of occurrence. What you want to factor into your plans is the worst probable scenario. In order to for-

mulate this picture of the downside, you need to answer the following questions:

- What is the data suggesting about the most likely undesirable outcome?
- What would the likely unfavorable environment be like?
- What is the probability of this happening?

Describe this scenario clearly, honestly, and accurately. Don't exaggerate or underestimate the real possibilities. And once again, drill below the surface of the negative outcome to pinpoint the contributing factors or variables at the root level that could cause or account for this less fortunate result.

> "The taste for worst-case scenarios reflects the need to master fear of what is felt to be uncontrollable. It also expresses an imaginative complicity with disaster."
> *Susan Sontag*
> *American Author and Human Activist*

If you have complex targets and want to explore more scenarios, it is okay. Sometimes there may be an unusual, creative, or different scenario lurking out there. These may be more difficult to describe. They may be hybrids, or a mix of positive and negative outcomes. Describe these unusual scenarios to the best of your ability, and once again try to look at the causal factors (independent variables) that could produce the creative or unique story line of the future.

The range and number of scenarios are clearly up to you. Keep in mind that the scenarios change and evolve over time. As new data comes in, you can revise or recreate the scenarios. You can always check the data and revise the probability ratings. Avoid getting bogged down at this stage of the process. Remember your strategic analysis should guide you and free you to decide and act, not paralyze you.

> "Remember, your strategic analysis should guide you and free you to act, not paralyze you."

As you formulate your scenarios, you will likely have two choices. Choice number one is to stay put for the moment, until the scenarios are more favorable, or to gather more information before making a decision. Choice number two is to move forward, go deeper, and continue to pursue the target by mapping out a specific course of action.

One of the managers we interviewed during our research described how valuable strategic thinking was to her. As she shared her experience, you could see how practical the scenarios that she had created could be. Mary was a very successful branch manager in mid career. She was known for her ability to organize, motivate, and turn troubled branches into successful operations. The company came to Mary and asked her to turn around a troubled branch in Arizona. Mary lived in Denver, so she would have to move to Arizona for nine months because the problems were very serious and needed a great deal of attention.

At this particular branch in Arizona, two sexual harassment charges had been filed, profitability was the lowest in the region, and recent surveys indicated that morale was at an all-time low. Because of the geographic distance, and since the only other branch manager in Arizona was new to the job, it didn't make a lot of sense to combine the offices.

Given the situation, the company did what it had always done; call on Mary to bail them out. However, this time something was different, and Mary could see it coming. Mary decided that "she" should be the target of her strategic thinking. She needed to focus her energies on the "you" part of the strategic dashboard we referred to earlier.

In addition to being a talented leader, Mary was a talented single mother of two. Her son was a high school freshman doing well in sports but struggling in a couple of subject areas. Her daughter was younger and had finally established a circle of good friends that would be difficult to replace in a new city. In the past,

Mary was quick to move to the location of the troubled branches she worked with so she could stay long enough to overhaul the entire business.

Her current Denver assignment was a great success for her. She had been the branch manager for eighteen months in Denver, and it was her toughest and most demanding turnaround to date. It had been an exciting venture. But it had taken a toll on her with the stress of being a single mother, the business, and working on her MBA.

Mary strategically sensed that her current lifestyle was taking a toll both psychologically and physically. Her "intelligence" radar had indicated some data about herself and she was sensitive to the scenarios that came to mind. She knew that if she succeeded in Arizona her future career would be set, and she could become an area director with the wealth and security her family needed. But as she identified her resources and the forces swirling around her, she knew she needed to think through the situation. She couldn't leap into it. She studied the information and was able to decipher possible scenarios or eventualities. In fact, it wasn't the worst case scenario that bothered her, but the "worst probable" scenario.

As she honestly analyzed all of the data available to her, she could make a reasonably accurate prediction and the worst "probable" scenario didn't look good: burn out, serious health problems, an unhappy and struggling family, and a degree on hold. Yet, ironically, she knew in her heart that she could successfully turn the business around.

In her mind, she could see it: a business success and a "train wreck" for her personal life. As she considered all of the forces, her strengths and limitations, her personal intelligence data from doctors and counselors, she decided to carefully reflect on the eventualities. After defining the scenarios, she considered three choices:

1. Walk away from the assignment, let the company figure out another approach, and take a risk on her future career. 2. Take the assignment, move her family, and hope for the best. After all, she made it through before. 3. Propose an entirely new course of action, negotiate some major modifications in the assignment, and gather support from the company, family, and University. If these conditions weren't met, she would quietly walk away.

Because she could see the scenarios, Mary chose solution number three. It was a difficult negotiation, but she was clear in her mind that she would do it only if the plan was on her terms. By clearly thinking about the scenarios or end points, she was able to make a good choice and chart a future course of action that reflected the signals, concerns, hazards, risks, and opportunities. It took longer to set up the right course of action, but it all paid off:

1. She got Human Resources to commit to find a permanent manager within six months, rather than the customary twelve.

2. Mary's father agreed to move to Denver for six months to help with the family.

3. The University agreed to put her MBA degree on hold.

4. She would live in an apartment in Tucson for three days a week and manage from home via computer and conference calls two days a week.

> "A successful person is one who can lay a firm foundation with bricks that others throw at him or her."
>
> *David Brinkley*
> *U.S. Broadcast*
> *Journalist*

This outcome was only achieved with a lot of courage, creativity, and clarity in Mary's thinking. She knew that even this strategy had some risks: three days on site may not be enough, her children might not accept their grandfather as a temporary parental substitute, and her career would hit a wall if the turnaround didn't happen. But she could also see that if she didn't chart a unique course,

the stress would be unbearable, and her career track would come to a screeching halt anyway; not a good scenario.

CONCLUSION

Scenarios begin the process of bringing the future into perspective. This enables you to look ahead in the face of uncertainty and lay the groundwork for future action. The scenarios, based on intelligence and analysis of external and internal forces, prepare you for whatever lies ahead.

Defining a scenario doesn't have to be difficult. When you stop and think about scenarios, you may notice that they are going through your mind and unfolding around you all of the time. In other words, you are seeing the results of historical scenarios unfold today. You may not have articulated or defined the scenarios in the past, but you could have. In fact, you can work backwards and actually define the key events and sequence of factors that led you to your current job, your current success level, your career path, etc. We like to call these the "backward" looking scenarios. This is really good practice when it comes to learning how to construct future scenarios. If you can figure out where you were and what got you where you are now, you can, in all likelihood, learn to project forward and determine likely future states and what will cause them to occur.

> "There are risks and costs to a program of action. But they are far less than the long-range risks and costs of comfortable inaction."
>
> *John F. Kennedy*
> *35th President of*
> *the United States*

Conversely, you can get others around you to project scenarios and compare them with what you foresee happening in the future. This comparison will enable you to calculate or theorize more accurately how the future will turn out and what will produce a particular end result.

CHAPTER NINE

Chart a Course

9

Chart a Course

Have you ever traveled through a long, dark tunnel? The Eisenhower Tunnel is the highest vehicular tunnel in the world, with a maximum elevation of 11,158 feet above sea level. The tunnel traverses through the Continental Divide within the Arapaho National Forest located in the Central Rockies of North America and is 1.693 miles long. Because of its length, you can't see the light at the end until you are a great distance into the tunnel, but you enter it knowing that you will come to the end. So it can be, in some situations, with applied strategic thinking.

"See strategy as important; have detailed implementation plans; and use strategy to help identify what to stop doing."

Anonymous

Now, contrast the tunnel analogy with that of a jungle. Instead of having a very specific or narrow strategic course to travel, you may be confronted with a jungle to navigate through. Some jungles, also known as rain forests, have the most biologically diverse ecosystems in the world. They account for less than 7% of the Earth's land surface, yet they contain more than 50% of its plant and animal life. Rain forests are distinct from other forests because they have layers of vegetation known as strata. These layers and canopies cause jungles to be thick and dense, and in some cases, very dark and difficult to navigate. You may find yourself with a strategic course of action that will take you into a thick jungle and a diverse ecosystem to contend with. In a strategic jungle, you will confront unexpected

situations and have to do a lot of work to traverse through the strata in order to reach your strategic target. A strategic course like this is very different from a "tunnel" type of plan.

Creating a Course of Action

Whether you must travel through a tunnel or a jungle, the next step in the strategic thinking process is defining the path and charting a course that will help you reach your target. Charting a course is the culmination of all the work you have done; it moves you into the execution and mobilization stage of strategy. Fundamentally, charting a course is knowing what you need to accomplish and defining the specific list of action steps that will lead you to your destination. This list includes what you will, might, or should do: specific tasks, assignments, time frames, and other important details that will move you forward. In addition to action steps, you might include a series of intermediate goals that need to be met in order to reach your target. Clearly defined plans contain markers, mileposts, or indicators of progress. They will also help you locate potential shortcuts, dangers, or other variables in your journey. A course of action is vitally important to prevent you from going off course as you pursue your strategic target. Remember, it won't always be perfect, and it will need to be adjusted as you execute it. If the water gets rough and choppy, you can always trim your sails and look for an alternative way through the obstacle.

> "Charting a course is the culmination of all the work you have done; it moves you into the execution and mobilization stage of strategy."

To chart a course, find a time and place where you can think clearly and brainstorm. As you sit down at your drawing board, consider the specific resources you will need and formulate specific actions for developing opportunities, leveraging strengths, responding to threats, and overcoming weaknesses. Focus on actions that will generate decisive results, and explore creative and innovative possibilities. As you do this, identify concrete mileposts that will help you monitor your progress. Be specific, because ambiguity at this stage will create a lot of confusion later on. Continue to rely on your intelligence and other information you identified as you advanced throughout the process to this point.

Major Obstacles or Hazards

As you scope out the various steps that will move you toward your target, pinpoint the major obstacles or hazards that could derail your plan. These are the potholes or obstructions in the tunnel that will give you a flat tire or the unknown territory and hazards in the jungle that will cause you to get lost. Think preemptively about what you can do to avoid these challenges altogether or how you can move through them if you have to. You  may have identified many of these factors as you gathered intelligence and analyzed forces. At this stage you can utilize the thinking and work you have already completed and orchestrate the implementation of specific actions that will drive you forward.

Inevitably, you will face challenges and obstacles along the path that you may or may not be able to plan for. We have always been impressed with the online map services that you can use for driving directions and estimated travel time. The directions from these services always seem to be clear and accurate, as is also true with a good strategic course of action. In only one situation did we encounter a few small problems that had an impact on our  travel to a client's location. The first involved estimated travel time. The time that the directions forecasted would normally have been correct; however, we encountered extensive road construction that we were unaware of until we saw the road construction signs. The second problem we ran into related to a small jog in the road and a turn signal that had recently been added. This jog

in the road put us onto the wrong road, and we missed a turn altogether. During this journey, we discovered that despite an excellent road map, we faced some challenges and obstacles along the way that we had to confront on the spot. Anything you can do before your journey begins to alleviate similar problems, which includes having good intelligence and thoroughly analyzing your threats and opportunities, will improve the likelihood of your success. But you may still encounter problems you are unable to or can't anticipate. In these situations, contingency plans are necessary and should include the signals that will indicate you have gone off course or encountered a problem.

> "You may still encounter problems that you were unable to or can't anticipate."

Most automobiles now have warning lights and indicators on the dashboard. We have heard these referred to as "idiot lights." They warn you about low fuel levels, engine problems, oil levels, maintenance needs, etc. We often rely on these indicators as we drive around, and you may too. As you relate our reliance on warning lights to strategic thinking, these indicators are anything but idiotic. Actually, relying on indicators is extremely smart! As you travel on your strategic journey, you will have greater success if you have thoroughly charted your course and have indicators in place. With such indicators, you will have been as intelligent and thorough as you can be in planning any strategic journey.

Strategic Opportunities

Similar plans and indicators for strategic opportunities will prepare you to quickly seize and capitalize on these opportunities by unleashing your resources at the appropriate time. Your course of action should thoroughly utilize and leverage your strengths. Shape your plans to play to your strengths and to neutralize your weaknesses whenever possible. Think outside of the box with new innovations, and the

effects will be astonishing when it comes time to activate the plan.

Necessary Resources

Once you have begun investigating the action steps that will likely lead you to your strategic target, you will also want to ex-amine the resources, provisions, or means that will be required for your journey. Consider what you will need in your shopping cart. As you plot out your plan, make a list of both tangible and intangible re-sources. In some cases, you may find that you already have the resources in your inventory and in other cases you may need to find ways to obtain the resources.

Typical resources include:

• Machinery or equipment	• Time
• Tools	• People
• Books and readings	• Information
• Material	• Knowledge
• Technology	• Training
• Money	• Advisors

If you are traveling through a jungle instead of a tunnel, you will want to do your homework so you know how to be as prepared as possible. Then plan the specific resources and supplies you will need for survival. You may also find yourself looking for resources along your journey—"living off the land" so to speak.

It is critical to make sure that your resources are not obsolete or in disrepair. This reminds us of the movie "Ocean's Eleven." There is a scene in this movie where the thieves have nearly reached the safe that holds their strategic target (millions of dollars), only to find that the batteries are dead in one of the important resources for opening the safe. The one

says to the other, "Didn't you check the batteries?" Before venturing into your own tunnels and jungles, make sure you have checked the batteries!

If you find yourself with a long list of resources, identify the primary or essential resources and then the secondary or desirable resources. Use these categories to help you zero in on which resources are essential for the journey. If you find that you have resource gaps, begin to analyze how and when you can fill those gaps. With many strategic initiatives, the inability to obtain resources can be a roadblock to moving forward. Use your creativity and innovation to identify alternative resources and substitutes that may prove to be more fruitful or that can fill gaps where resources may be hard to come by. Think of it as a recipe for a delicious dessert. Sometimes we may elect to use a substitute instead of an alternative, yet we can still have a culinary masterpiece.

> "Great emergencies and crises show us how much greater our vital resources are than we had supposed.
>
> *William James*
> *U.S. Philosopher and*
> *Psychologist*

A "S.M.A.R.T." Plan

When you reach a point where you feel you have created a strong framework for a course of action, review the steps and make your plan S.M.A.R.T. (Specific, Measurable, Attainable, Relevant, and Timebound). It should include roles, responsibilities, assignments, and due dates. This will help ensure that the plan is specific enough to really define how you will complete your journey and how you will know if you have succeeded. Clarify how you will maintain accountability and discipline for each action step. Accountability and discipline will become the mechanisms for continuing forward in the strategic

> "What we anticipate seldom occurs; what we least expect generally happens."
>
> *Benjamin Disraeli*
> *British Prime*
> *Minister and*
> *Novelist*

adventure. Your plan doesn't necessarily have to be complex or large. It should carefully match the size and scope of your strategic target. As you review the course you have charted, double check the time and costs involved in each step so you are sure you have accurately prepared for your journey.

Some broad examples of action steps might include the following:

X	Action Step	Measurement	Responsibility	Due Date
	Identify high-potential vendors.			
	Contact high-potential vendors to schedule demonstrations.			
	Develop a list of criteria for evaluation.			
	Visit other departments for benchmarking.			
	Review the budget for possible adjustments.			
	Talk with team members about availability and to explain the strategic target.			
	Research the cost benefit of the new approach vs. an alternative approach.			
	Build a list of customers who will be impacted in the future.			
	Prepare an e-mail that explains upcoming changes to customers.			

Using a simple table or grid for your action steps with space for notes, responsibilities, timeframes, etc. will be extremely valuable in ensuring you deliberately execute each action step.

Communicating the Plan

A final, but critical step in charting your course is communicating it to key players, passengers, and anyone else involved in the strategic journey. A good question to ask yourself is, "To whom does this strategic effort matter and why?" Articulate the plan to these people, and be open to their feedback or ideas. You may find that others can enhance the course of action or fill in any gaps you may have missed. Don't leave out the roles,

> "Be sure that your allies are aligned and empowered to fulfill their responsibilities."

responsibilities, timelines, and accountability measures in your communications. Including key information will eliminate confusion and waste while enhancing coordinated effort. Be sure that your allies are aligned and empowered to fulfill their responsibili-

ties. If you are traveling through a tunnel, help them understand what is at the other end. If you are traveling into a jungle to reach your strategic target, help your partners understand the terrain and the difficult nature of the situation so there aren't any surprises when the path gets murky or ambiguous. Keep the communication lines open and help them understand the process for raising issues, concerns, or a need for other information throughout the journey. If these channels are open, you will find that your allies will help you activate and accelerate the plan in ways you might not have been able to foresee.

A carefully developed course of action will be critical in attaining your strategic initiative and giving you peace of mind. You have already come far in the strategic thinking process; spend the time necessary to explore your best route of travel so when fate meets preparation ...you win! Don't get caught venturing into a long, dark tunnel or through a dense jungle without the plans and resources that will lead you through the terrain that lies ahead.

Planning Brings Your Future

It isn't enough just to want something.
You've got to ask yourself,
"What am I going to do to get the things that I want?"
You're going to need a plan.

Your problem is to bridge the gap which exists
Between where you are right now
And the goals that you want to reach.
With a definite, step by step plan, you cannot fail,
Because each step will carry you along to the next step,
like a track.

All you need is the plan, the road map,
and the courage to press on to your destination.
Knowing where you're going is key to getting there.

You shouldn't get lost on a straight road.

— Unknown

"Luck is a
crossroad where
preparation and
opportunity meet."
Anonymous

CHAPTER TEN

Mobilize and Sustain

10

Mobilize and Sustain

By now you are well into the strategic process. You have done a lot of work, and hopefully you are excited about the course you have mapped out. The plan you created should produce the strategic success that you are hoping to achieve. Now you are ready to begin marching as unerringly as possible until you have achieved as much of the target as possible. Remember, your strategic target isn't going to magically show up on your doorstep as a result of intense thinking or wishing. The one step between thinking about what you want and actually getting it is action. There is an ancient saying; "The journey of a thousand miles begins with a single step." And so it is with mobilizing your strategy. All you have to do is muster enough motivation to get moving. Hopefully the prospect of achieving the strategic target that you now have in your sights will produce enough initial energy to launch you into the action. So now, let's turn our attention to the principles that will allow you to effectively act and execute your plans.

"Your strategic target isn't going to magically show up on your doorstep as result of thinking or wishing."

There are seven principles and skills that will get your expedition successfully launched and move you along the path to your strategic target on the horizon.

Mobilization Principle #1: Overcome Fear of Failure

Most people falsely assume that a lack of time is the biggest stumbling block to doing something that is truly strategic. In reality, fear of failure and of making mistakes is one of the biggest impediments to real progress. If you think that you are not going to make some mistakes, don't bother trying to be strategic. Elbert Hubbard said, "The greatest mistake you can make in life is continually fearing you will make one." When developing formulas for successful execution, mistakes and setbacks are usually left out of the equations. However, missing the mark or coming up short is all part of the strategic process. Mistakes are inevitable. It is very possible that many of your short-term failures will help you achieve the long-term benefits of your strategic campaign. Success over the long haul depends on sustained effort and learning, which means that from time to time you are going to miss the mark. You must develop the capacity to turn short-term and tactical failures into valuable learning opportunities. These situations will enable you to make adjustments and move forward. A worthwhile and rewarding strategic target requires a willingness to receive and process failure effectively. There is no way that you will talk yourself into taking a strategic risk unless you know how to fail effectively.

> "Fear of failure and of making mistakes is one of the biggest impediments to real progress."

The key is to leverage failure, to treat failure as a stepping stone and not as something that will stop your progress. To do this, most people have to bridle their intense desire to be perfect or to be successful at every point on the voyage. Again, the focus should be on learning and introspection. A friend of ours calls it a "little learn." When Yvonne makes a mistake, she constantly reminds herself that it was a "little learn." She captures the point, has an internal

> "Life's real failure is when you do not realize how close you were to success when you gave up."
> *Anonymous*

debriefing of the mistake, and then makes a mental note of how to avoid it next time. Or she goes back to the drawing board and comes up with a modification plan to keep herself moving.

It has been said that when NASA selects astronauts, the candidates not only need experience and technical qualifications, but they also need significant experience with failure and the ability to bounce back from setbacks. NASA leaders apparently believe that a person who failed but then got up again and tried would be better suited for the work than someone who had never learned how to fail effectively. Periodically you should conduct a strategy review to identify what is working and what isn't so you can make smart adjustments in your course of action. Be adaptable and flexible because failure leads to new opportunities and innovations; it doesn't have to be an ending point.

> "You can't tell how deep a puddle is until you step into it."
>
> *Anonymous*

Mobilization Principle #2: Take Incremental Steps

Sometimes just the idea of doing something strategic sounds big and daunting. To counteract the appearance of something intimidating, break the plan down into incremental parts and concentrate your energy in these areas. Hopefully you created some specific, incremental steps when you mapped out a course of action, so the key to success is to attack the high-priority or the high-payoff elements of the plan and put a few points on the board. It is very easy to get excited about the new directions you are taking yourself or your team, and you may be tempted to undertake too many actions. It is far better to select a few actions you can legitimately support and focus on, rather than tackling a lot of activities that are poorly supported with time, energy, or money. Military strategists understand this better than anyone; you don't want to pick a fight you can't

> "Select a few actions you can legitimately support and focus on."

win. Instead, approach each task you have selected with an over-whelming force and win decisively.

Select one thing from the course of action that you can begin working on. Obviously, it should be something within your sphere of control, something that plays to the strengths you identified earlier in the strategic thinking process. Small steps are appropriate at this point; in fact, the whole idea is to find the point of attack that will demonstrate some progress and reaffirm your commitment to the plan.

Remember, being out in front with your actions makes you a target for second-guessing and ridicule by others who are less courageous. Fear of separation from your group can be a very real thing. Don't randomly and fanatically attack everything. Pick your targets, and move steadily and confidently forward in a few areas. Being more strategic requires courage and nerve in order to make consistent progress.

Mobilization Principle #3: Make a Commitment

Nothing will ever happen unless you have had a conversation with yourself about commitment. Commitment is more than a decision to do something. It is deeper. Commitment is a personal belief that has been internalized to the point that you don't have to think about it. In other words, the strategic target is part of you. It defines who you are and what you are about. Commitment means that you are not afraid to talk about your target and your strategic plan with others. The target is something that you have grown to value deeply and about which you are unwilling to compromise. Once you have made a

> "There's a difference between interest and commitment. When you're interested in doing something, you do it only when circumstances permit. When you're committed to something, you accept not excuses, only results."
>
> *Anonymous*

decision to do something and you really believe it, amazing things can happen. Providence moves in, and all sorts of unforeseen incidents and assistance occur. When others around you begin to sense your intentions, you create a magnet for good things, a belief that you are serious. A sense of commitment doesn't mean that everything will come together perfectly right now, but it does mean that you are resolute and determined.

Mobilization Principle #4: Pick Up Speed

A successful track coach once told us that you can't teach speed. In some situations that is probably true, but one thing we have observed from both interviews and workshops on strategy is that strategic people know when to take their foot off the analytical brake pedal and accelerate. Now, this doesn't mean that you need to recklessly accelerate through every part of the course of action that you have mapped out. But it does mean that you can selectively prioritize the high-leverage activities that you can afford to do now. The key is to move out rapidly in these areas, to put some important aspects of your plan of action in gear. The worst thing you can do is sit back and wait for the ideal moment to launch the quest.

> "We live in a moment of history where change is so speeded up that we begin to see the present only when it is already disappearing."
>
> *R. D. Laing*
> *Scottish Psychiatrist*

Nothing will motivate you more than if you get a quick start. Fast action demonstrates to others who may be waiting and second guessing that you are serious about your intentions. John Lyly once said, "Delays breed dangers."

Mobilization Principle # 5: Be Responsive

As you mobilize your strategy, you will regularly use knowledge, information, and the signals about opportunities and threats that you put into place earlier in the process. Fully utilize these mechanisms to adapt and to be responsive so you don't get delayed by roadblocks. It is easy to get caught up in the specific plan, the one that you are committed to, that you are not flexible enough to make large or even small adjustments along the road. Improvise and be creative in response to the variety of circumstances you encounter along the path. Collaborate with others and create synergies with key allies to learn how you can most effectively adapt and adjust. Continuously measuring your progress is another important aspect of this journey. The quantitative or qualitative data that is used to monitor your progress will enable you to quickly know if you are on track or off track, or if some other adjustments are needed to fully execute your plan.

Mobilization Principle # 6: Demonstrate Resolve

As you venture out on your strategic odyssey, you must have the internal discipline and fortitude to stay cool and to persist over time. Resolve means follow through on your action plans. Strategic success requires a lot more than the euphoria that occurs when you select a target and chart a course. It is easy to get overly ambitious and bite off more than you can chew. So you need to size up the specific task or activity and realistically allocate your assets and resources so you can sustain the entire implementation process. You have to demonstrate to everyone around you that you have the courage to lead the change and keep the campaign alive long-term, even in the face of adversity. Once you chart your course, it is time to mount a disciplined attack and finish the task. Without question, you will experience trials and reversals along the path to your solution or target. You have to be willing to support and invest in your strategy when you experience upsets and letdowns. Strategy is never achieved unless there is exertion, follow through, and drive.

> "Frequently, the difference between success and failure is the resolve to stick to your plan long enough to win."
>
> *David Cottrell*
> *Author*

Mobilization Principle # 7: Instill Teamwork

The battle of Waterloo began when the French started four attacks against the British army. The intent was to weaken the center so the French could break through. However, the attacks by the French failed because there was no coordinated teamwork between the French infantry and cavalry. With most strategic endeavors, the coordinated effort and assistance of others are required to fully carry out your strategy. If successful execution requires team members, partners, allies, etc., you will want to gain commitment to manage resistance from these key players and build a common understanding  of your strategic vision. So often, though, key allies do not understand the overall strategy and their responsibility in achieving it, nor are they empowered with the authority to fulfill their assignments. Value your allies and partners. Set them up for success so they can deliver success for you.

> "Value your allies and partners. Set them up for success so they can deliver success for you."

Sled dogs have an inbred trait to run. However, they have to be taught to run harmoniously by a dedicated driver called a musher. A team of sled dogs working together can pull a sled and person for hundreds of miles. As you launch your strategy, ensure that you have fully prepared, aligned, and equipped your team to "stay the course." As the "musher" of your team, you can utilize their strengths and abilities to lead you to success.

CONCLUSION

Mobilizing your strategy is your "call to battle stations." All along, we have talked about getting more strategic about your operations and not getting into the operational trap. Now it is time to get operational about your strategy. You may not be able to devote every waking moment to the pursuit of your target, but you will need to be rigorous and doggedly committed to doing something about it on a regular basis. Now is the time to take the plunge. You have probably demonstrated that you can perform in the "operational zone" of the strategic terrain. Now you are in a position to go beyond performance or success and achieve significance.

> "Build for your team a feeling of oneness, of dependence on one another and of strength to be derived by unity."
> *Vince Lombardi*
> *U.S. Football Coach*

When it comes right down to it, strategy only works when it is implemented. Mobilization is simply putting the plan in play piece-by-piece. At this stage, you need to be fired up. You know there will be some setbacks with strategy implementation. Remember that failure is more about attitude than it is about outcome. Successful strategists have their minds locked on, are determined, and are ready to discipline their routines to make room in their lives for strategy. They seem to have the attitude that they would rather die bloody on the strategic battlefield than continue to plod away in the world of the routine.

If you want to be strategic you have to be ready for a long march. It isn't like an operational change or event. Strategic change is deeper. It requires some fundamental retooling of the way you operate. It requires a clear plan to sustain the effort. This is different than a clear plan to launch the strategy. You will be successful in the long haul if you have a clear target, a clear path, and a clear sustaining strategy.

CHAPTER ELEVEN

The Future

11

The Future

The future is similar to a complex battlefield, and each of us has our own with many fronts. Most of the time we are engaged and occupied with immediate challenges moment by moment. Yet we envision these battles much like the  Italian Paredo: 80% of the battle action will determine only 20% of your success, and 20% will determine a whopping 80% of your success. The key is to find that critical 20% of your work and to approach it strategically. We believe that people can and should take the time, summon the courage, and put their minds on a strategic course more often.

There is no question that the future will be a wily and determined opponent. You are not likely to win every skirmish or battle, even with exceptional strategic thinking. But if you can improve your odds over time by using the process we have outlined, you will be better prepared and have a distinct advantage when you face important work and life battles.

With a clear head, good intelligence, thorough analysis, a course of action in mind, and discipline to stay the course you will be focused and battle tested like a Samurai warrior. Then, the only thing you will need is relentless courage and determination to go after your target and not give up.

Much of what we have learned about strategic thinking comes from interviews and

> "With a clear head, good intelligence, thorough analysis, a course of action in mind, and discipline to stay the course, you will be focused and battle tested like a Samurai warrior."

observations of successful individuals and from extensive reading on strategy. But our most important insights have come from actually using the process from a personal and work-related perspective. Like a lot of people, we have learned from experiences that in many cases we could have been more successful if only we had looked up and out at the horizon. These powerful lessons have crystallized an applied strategic thinking road map that has helped us control the future and tame the beast of day-to-day fire fighting.

For some, the future seems mysterious and illusive. It may seem too much to expect to become a more strategic leader or worker, or the future may seem pre-determined and out of your control. There is no question that some parts of the future appear extremely distant and are out of your sphere of influence. With all of the uncertainties out there, you will never feel completely prepared for what is in store for you. But that doesn't mean you can't anticipate and reduce the surprises that lie ahead. Being strategic means that you are agile and flexible when you encounter bumps in the road or when golden opportunities arrive. Why wouldn't you want to protect your investment in your profession,

> "Being strategic means that you are agile and flexible when you encounter bumps in the road or when golden opportunities arrive."

your career, and your job? As we have indicated, you need to rely on your talents and strengths to lead you into the future and to

 help you decide which battles to engage in and when you should "skate fast" to avoid letting a weakness tow you under. You need to be strategic, because in the final analysis life comes at you fast. If you are not prepared, you are subject to fate's whims. It is worth repeating again: you have to be strategic so when fate meets your preparation, you win!

If others in your organization or on your team notice your strategic behavior and thought process, it will ignite the entrepreneurial spirit in others, and it will become part of the organization's

fabric. Imagine the possibilities if even a few more people in your group had a sense of being entrepreneurial and were strategically aligned on some shared targets. Imagine the value that could be created for customers if more people were poised

and positioned to exploit the future better. Some people tell us

> **"The future influences the present just as much as the past."**
> *Friedrich Nietzsche*
> *German Philosopher*
> *and Writer*

that they can't decide whether or not to adopt a more strategic way of thinking or style of working. The fact is that if you do not choose to take on the future more deliberately, you are choosing to live in the past or to live moment-to-moment. You are choosing to stay with the status quo rather than to be an agent for change. In short, "failing to prepare can mean preparing to fail." If you don't proactively create or lay the groundwork for tomorrow's opportunities and solutions today, who will?

Don't be hard on yourself when you get it wrong, have a setback, or your predictions are off the mark. Remember that the strategic process is fluid. Each day the battle plan gets a little better, the intelligence improves, and you learn more because your mind is operating from a strategic vantage point.

The essence of applied strategy is preparing you for your new or enhanced contribution. It is a lot more than just preparing you to be more efficient in performing your current activities. Being strategic is all about taking that "new" stride forward, figuring out what that new stride is, and when and how to take it. This means moving in different directions and creating different roles to play in your work.

We have acknowledged that while this shift in perspective is going on, you will have to deal with a lot. You will have to struggle to become more efficient and to elevate your current performance while you are searching for direction in your future life and learning how to have both impact and meaning. Without question,

being strategic involves a different way of looking at your work. It is all very relative when you begin to scope out the future, to discover ways to position yourself to add value to your organization and meaning to your life down the road. Some people see the future as a long way off and believe that the future will somehow take care of itself. However, in some situations or on some tasks, the future is very near, and what is important is literally weeks or days ahead. In other cases, the future means years. The future is a very relative thing; it is all very situational. In reality, a timeframe is irrelevant when you are looking beyond the present moment, when you are looking beyond the parameters of the current problem. When you are considering future ramifications, you are operating in the domain of strategy.

"If a great thing can be done, it can be done easily, but this ease is like the ease of a tree blossoming after long years of gathering strength."

John Ruskin
English Writer and
Critic

Don't let the word "strategy" fool you or the future scare you. You have carefully studied some tools and examples in this book that will help you navigate

gate through the future. Practice makes perfect, so actively use these skills. The future isn't as far away as you think! Hopefully we have provided some useful food for thought as you chart your voyage beyond the present and into the future.

The
APPLIED STRATEGIC THINKING
Workshop

Why a workshop on Applied Strategic Thinking?

S trategic thinking is sometimes viewed as a complex and intimidating topic. However, thinking strategically is simply having the skills and foresight to solve tomorrow's problems today. We believe that this kind of strategic thinking can benefit leaders and teams in all types of organizations, as well as the individual who wants to truly ignite positive change.

The Applied Strategic Thinking Workshop will teach participants how to think, plan, and act more strategically at the individual level and on the front lines of work. Through real life experiences, illustrated examples, straightforward activities, and tools, the Applied Strategic Thinking Workshop outlines the necessary skills to become strategically minded and forward thinking.

Participants Will Learn How To:
- Define "Applied Strategic Thinking" and the principles that go with it.
- Develop the skills necessary to think and act at a strategic level.
- Align and link the individual strategy with organizational strategy.
- Identify and exploit opportunities.
- Analyze strengths and weaknesses.
- Successfully capitalize on forces and events that shape their life and work.
- Gather and use intelligence data.
- Analyze the changes happening today that will influence tomorrow's results.
- Accelerate and sustain strategic initiatives.

Workshop—One Day Version:
- What is Strategic Thinking?
- Exercise—Why strategic thinking needs to be one of the centerpieces of everyone's responsibilities?
- The Applied Strategic Thinking Model and Key Skills.
- Strategic Thinking Assessment.
- The Applied Strategic Thinking Model In-Depth.
- Exercise—Why it is important to plan and map out your future.
- Practice applying the principles and skills.
- Design action plans.

How the Workshop is Offered

The Applied Strategic Thinking Workshop can be delivered in a one, two, and two and a half-day format. The two and a half-day workshop is conducted at one of the greatest historic sites in the United States, the Gettysburg Battleground. The Applied Strategic Workshop can be tied directly to the battlefield strategies used at Gettysburg. Participants will spend part of the workshop exploring the battlefield with an expert tour guide, while our facilitator relates the points of the tour to the workshop and the Applied Strategic Thinking Model. This innovative approach to the workshop delivery is an engaging and a once in a lifetime experience for participants.

Other books from CMOE Press

Win Win Partnerships: Be on the Leading Edge with Synergistic Coaching

The Coach: Creating Partnerships for a Competitive Edge

The Team Approach: With Teamwork Anything Is Possible

Teamwork: We Have Met the Enemy and They Are Us

Leading Groups to Solutions: A practical guide for facilitators and team members.

To order call (801) 569-3444 or visit www.cmoe.com

About CMOE

The Center for Management and Organization Effectiveness (CMOE) was founded in 1978 with the vision and mission to help organizations improve leadership and team member skills. We have grown into a powerful strategic partner with organizations worldwide over the past two decades by consistently meeting client needs. Through in-depth research and consulting, CMOE has developed highly effective, skill-based training programs, workshops, materials, and experiences that address the specific needs of individuals and organizations. CMOE continues to develop customized courses for our clients that make an impact on the leaders and team members of today and tomorrow. We have successfully designed and delivered programs for a variety of Fortune 500 companies, as well as smaller organizations. In our commitment to developing long-term relationships, we find that our clients are often introduced to CMOE through one program, and then identify other programs that will help them address additional needs. A sample of our clients follows:

- Chevron
- Boeing
- Dun & Bradstreet
- PepsiCo
- Federal Express
- Procter & Gamble

- FMC Corporation
- Pacific Gas and Electric
- Exxon Mobil
- Phillips Petroleum
- Motorola